Compiled & edited by Ken Ham & Bodie Hodge

BEGIN ▶

a journey through

scriptures for seekers

and new believers

Master
Books®
A Division of New Leaf Publishing Group
www.masterbooks.net

First printing: July 2011
Seventh printing: April 2013

ISBN: 978-0-89051-630-0
Library of Congress Number: 2011930778

Cover by Diana Bogardus

Connecting material between selected books "What does it mean to be saved?" "Wasn't the Bible Written by Mere Men?" and "Why Don't Christians Follow all the Old Testament Laws?" is by Bodie Hodge. "Ten Basics" section is by various Answers in Genesis staff.

Please consider requesting that a copy of this volume be purchased by your local library system.

Printed in the United States of America

Please visit our website for other great titles:
www.masterbooks.net

For information regarding author interviews,
please contact the publicity department at (870) 438-5288

Master
Books®
A Division of New Leaf Publishing Group
www.masterbooks.net

Dedication

We dedicate this book to those people who want to know more about the Christian faith and seek answers to questions that create doubt in their minds regarding the Bible's trustworthiness. With this book we have set out to give an overview of the Bible so that our readers can obtain a "big picture" understanding of the Bible's thrust and meaning.

We should not be afraid to ask questions, but we should all be willing to seek and then listen to the answers presented in God's Word.

The two of us would also like to dedicate this book to the Ham and Hodge families for supporting and helping us in our endeavor to further the proclamation of the gospel of Jesus Christ. It is to Him whom we seek to give all honor and glory.

— Ken and Bodie

Contents

Foreword 6

A Brief Introduction 8

Genesis 1–11: A Brief Commentary to Get You Started 10

Scripture: Genesis 1–11 16

A Brief Review of History from Abram to Moses
and the Ten Commandments 50

Scripture: Exodus 20 52

A Brief Review of History from the Ten Commandments
to Christ 54

Scripture: John 1–21 58

From the Ascension of Christ to Paul's Letter to the Romans 142

Scripture: Romans 1–4 144

Why Don't Christians Follow all the Old Testament Laws? 158

Scripture: Romans 5–8 160

Who Created God? 169

Scripture: Romans 9–16 170

From Paul's Letter to the Romans to John's Vision
of the Apocalypse (Revelation) 192

Scripture: Revelation 21–22 194

What Does It Mean to Be Saved? 200

Ten Basics to Boldly Proclaim a Biblical Worldview 210

    1. Six Literal Days 211

    2. Radiometric Dating 213

    3. Variety within Created Kinds 216

    4. Uniqueness of Man 218

    5. Distant Starlight 220

    6. Global Flood 222

    7. Dinosaurs on the Ark 224

    8. One Race 226

    9. Suffering and Death 229

   10. The Gospel 231

A Final Note of Truth: Wasn't the Bible Written
    by Mere Men? 234

Foreword

Many Christians today are passing out copies of the New Testament (which often include the Psalms and Proverbs from the Old Testament) in their effort to share God's Word with others. Of course, that is a wonderful idea, but I suggest there is now an increasing problem with this approach. You see, most people who receive these New Testaments have been trained by the secular world, which comes through the influence of the news media, movies, Internet, public schools, and even many Christian schools/colleges, to believe in evolution and millions of years. They have been taught a set of foundational beliefs that cause them to doubt or even totally disbelieve the truth of God's Word in Genesis. Ultimately, this creates doubt and disbelief in regard to the whole of the Bible, including the Gospel message of the New Testament.

When only the New Testament portion of the Bible is given to "evolutionized" people, they do not receive the Book of Genesis, which gives them the true account of origins. Genesis is foundational to an understanding of the gospel and all Christian doctrine. In this increasingly secularized culture, people no longer fully understand the gospel message and the origin of sin and death as found in Genesis — and thus our need of a Savior. Not only that, but because of what people have been taught in regard to origins, many have great doubts (or full-blown unbelief) that God's Word can be totally trusted.

When Christians pass out New Testaments and tell people they need to start with the Book of John to understand the gospel, something key is being missed. As people learn of the good news of the gospel, they also need to have an understanding of the bad news in Genesis: our sin in Adam, and that we are alienated from our Creator and are in need of a Savior. In today's world, people who read the New Testament only, by and large, rarely understand the gospel and the full meaning of the Christian faith because they have little understanding of the foundations of the gospel and how all Christian doctrine connects.

In addition, because of what people have been taught in their culture, as mentioned above, people are already skeptical about trusting the Bible they have been handed. In a culture that has little or no understanding of the Bible, Christians can be more effective when they start to share their faith at the beginning — in Genesis — so they will understand the Bible's full message of repentance and need for a Savior.

With this book, we decided to do something "radical." We have sought to give readers an overview of the Christian faith and the message of the gospel in the following manner: by presenting it the way God does it in His Word, and that's by starting at the Bible's beginning. In today's world, we need to communicate a message of the true God: our Creator God. Christians need to give the account of the true history of the world concerning creation, the first man and woman, the Fall of man, the entrance of sin and death, and the promise of the Savior fulfilled in the person of Jesus Christ. It is an essential approach to take in a world that knows little, for example, of the meaning and origin of sin, or why Christ, the Creator, stepped into history to be our Savior.

This book contains excerpts from God's Word beginning in Genesis to communicate a time-line of history from the beginning of time to Christ, and then to the New Heavens and New Earth to come. The Bible's message starting with Genesis is all about what God has done for the salvation of humankind. This book, using passages from Genesis to Revelation, seeks to give that vital message in summary form so that people will get a "big picture" understanding of the gospel — and be challenged to recognize their need of receiving Christ into their life as Lord and Savior.

I believe this book will be blessed by God to become a powerful evangelistic resource to reach a skeptical culture with the precious gospel message.

— Ken Ham

A Brief Introduction

The Bible is a big book — 66 books, to be exact. There are 39 in the Old Testament and 27 in the New Testament, and sometimes people get lost trying to read the whole Bible in many small segments. There are a number of reasons for this, such as reading genealogies, Levitical laws for the Israelites, poetic books, or the fact that some books of the Bible are simply not sitting in chronological order, which makes some readers lose focus.

In an effort to give readers a big picture of what the Bible is all about, from start to finish, we wanted to put together a few sections and books of the Bible to help readers get started — like an overview. This short segment of biblical texts is not meant to replace the Bible. The selected Scriptures are:

Genesis 1–11 (the Foundation)
Exodus 20:1–17 (the Ten Commandments)
John (the Gospel)
Romans (an Epistle or Letter from Paul to Christians)
Revelation 21–22 (the Fulfillment in Heaven)

There is a brief history of what happens between the various portions of Scripture that is meant to help the reader place each portion of Scripture. After one reads this book of selected Scriptures, our hope is that it helps one get excited about the Bible and its message as a whole, so one will go back and read the Bible to fill in even more details. After all, the entire Bible is inspired and inerrant, and no book is less important than others; we want to encourage our readers to read it all. Let's start at the beginning.

Genesis 1–11: A Brief Commentary to Get You Started

Genesis 1–11 is foundational to the rest of the Bible. It is the best place to start to understand doctrines of Christianity such as these:

+ Why we wear clothes
+ Why we suffer and die
+ Why God's perfect creation suddenly was cursed
+ Why the week is a 7-day period
+ Why we need a Savior
+ Why we need a new heavens and a new earth
+ Our reason for hope (it contains the first prophecy of Jesus, our Savior in Genesis 3:15)

Genesis 1–11 and the Four Evolution Ideas Forced on Most People

In short, Genesis 1–11 is the very beginning of all things. The beginning of time, space, and matter — and it is *God* who begins it all, not a random event of something popping into existence from nothing and rapidly exploding (e.g., the big bang as many have been taught, otherwise known as *astronomical evolution*).

Furthermore, God specially created growing and living things (plants on day 3, sea and flying creatures on day 5, and land animals and man on day 6.) Such things did not come about by random chemicals coming together and forming the first "life" (otherwise known as *chemical evolution*), the odds of which are virtually impossible anyway.

Genesis 1–11 refutes the idea that life evolved slowly over millions of years from one kind into another (amoeba to man, otherwise known as *biological evolution*). Animals, for example, were made according to their kind (which is not necessarily a *species* — it is probably closer to the *family* level by the modern classification system but not in all instances). There is a dog kind (including wolves, coyotes, dingoes, domestic dogs, etc.), a cat kind (including lions, tigers, bobcats, domestic cats, ligers, etc.), and an elephant kind (including Asian elephants, African elephants, mammoths, mastodons, etc.). There is variation among these but we don't observe one kind changing into another kind. Man was specially created from dust, not from "lower life forms," and when we die, we return to dust, not to some lower form of animal (Genesis 3:19).

Next, Genesis 1–11 refutes the idea of millions of years, otherwise known as *geological evolution*, for God created in six days, not in trillions of days (the idea of millions and billions of years). The idea of millions of years is recent. In the late 1700s and early 1800s, people began to leave the Bible out of the subject of origins and started looking at rock layers as though they were laid down slowly over millions of years — instead of by a global cataclysmic Flood! We can observe rock layers forming in floods and other catastrophes (e.g., volcanoes), yet we have never observed them forming over millions of years — ever! Genesis 6–8 discusses a yearlong global Flood that destroyed the earth and likely shifted continents and pushed up high mountains in continental collisions. Furthermore, a global Flood explains why some rock layers contain fossils.

Age of the Earth

God created over the course of six days and rested on the seventh in Genesis 1. The earth was made on the first creation day. Why six days? Exodus 20:11 explains that this a model for our workweek, and it also refutes the idea that a day in Genesis could be a long period of time. There is no need to downgrade what is written in the Bible to accommodate the secular evolutionary religion. (Evolution and millions of years are subsets of the religion of secular humanism, which is taught in most state schools, whereas creation is a subset of Christianity.) Many mistakenly assume that religion is not permitted in the classroom; however, when Christianity was kicked out of the classroom, religion wasn't. Christianity was replaced with a godless religion, that of secular humanism.

To continue, your and my grandpa, Adam, was created on the sixth day of creation. There are many genealogies in the Bible, and two sets of them are in Genesis 1–11. If you add up the genealogies from Adam to Abraham (see Genesis 5 and 11), you get about 2,000 years. Most scholars, whether Christian or secular, would say that Abraham lived about 2,000 years before Christ, which is about 4,000 years ago. A large number of chronologists have also arrived at numbers similar to this in their treatises. Arguably, the most popular is Archbishop James Ussher, who put the specific date of 4004 B.C. for creation. Sir Isaac Newton, arguably the greatest scientist who ever lived, affirmed this date and even did studies in the area of chronologies on his own.

Jesus also affirmed a younger age to the earth in Mark 10:6 when He said that God created man and woman (Adam and Eve) at the *beginning of creation*. On the sixth day is definitely at the beginning from the time Jesus made this statement (about 4,000 years later according to the genealogies) if the days are normal-length days. Had the creation been 13–15 billion years, as the secular humanists affirm (and sadly some Christian trust that over the Bible), then Jesus would have erred and should have stated the *end* of creation. But Christ's wording reveals that a younger earth is indeed what the Bible asserts, so 6,000 years indeed makes sense.

Long-Age Worldviews

Some Christians are pressured by the secular side and have bought into the idea of millions of years. Some of these positions that came about in the 1800s and 1900s are:

- Gap theory (inserting millions of years between Genesis 1:1 and 1:2)
- Day-age/progressive creation (taking the days of creation and stretching them out to be millions of years)
- Theistic evolution (do away with Genesis 1–11, replace it with an evolutionary worldview, and say God did it, then just pick up with Abraham).
- Framework hypothesis (really it is a modern variant of theistic evolution, giving early chapters of Genesis a literary style that allows it to be interpreted any way one chooses; leading developer of this view, Meredith Kline, held to an evolutionary worldview).

Each of these views takes humanism's ideas of millions of years as absolute and does not question them. So with these views, the Bible must be reinterpreted to accommodate this other religion's view of the age of the earth. One cannot fit millions of years in the genealogies from Christ to Adam. So they had no choice but to force the millions of years into Genesis 1 (creation week). But there are theological problems besides Exodus 20:11 and Mark 10:6.

The idea of millions of years came from the view of the rock layers. These rock layers contain dead things. Death, though, came as a result of sin — human sin with Adam. So how can millions of years of death be around prior to Adam sinning? It couldn't, so these dead things were fossilized after sin. The Flood of Noah's day makes perfect sense of these fossils. And note that these positions (gap, progressive theistic evolution, etc.) do not believe in a global Flood but instead appeal to a small local flood in the Middle East. Genesis 7:20 and Genesis 9:13–15 refute this idea of a local flood.

Furthermore, when God created, things were perfect (that is what we expect from a perfect God). This is found in Genesis 1:31 (everything was very good) and Deuteronomy 32:4 (every work of God is perfect). Had death, suffering, cancer, struggling, tumors, thorns, etc. (which we find in the fossil layers), existed before Adam and Eve sinned, then things would not have been very good and perfect. Otherwise these things would be very good and perfect, which they are not . . . as anyone who has had a family member die of cancer can attest.

There is a relationship between human sin and animal death. In Genesis 3:21, the Lord sacrificed animals to cover Adam's sin. In fact, in the whole of the Old Testament, people offered sacrifices for sin, and all this pointed toward Christ, the ultimate and final sacrifice to cover sins and offer mankind the opportunity to be saved from our sins (sins are roughly our disobedient actions and thoughts against God and others).

We hope these thoughts help you get started reading Genesis 1–11 and explain why they are so important in today's culture and to the rest of the Bible.

Genesis

The Creation of the World

1 In the beginning, God created the heavens and the earth. **2** The earth was without form and void, and darkness was over the face of the deep. And the Spirit of God was hovering over the face of the waters. **3** And God said, "Let there be light," and there was light. **4** And God saw that the light was good. And God separated the light from the darkness. **5** God called the light Day, and the darkness he called Night. And there was evening and there was morning, the first day.

FACT

God refutes atheism in the very first verse of Genesis.

6 And God said, "Let there be an expanse[1] in the midst of the waters, and let it separate the waters from the waters." **7** And God made[2] the expanse and separated the waters that were under the expanse from the waters that were above the expanse. And it was so. **8** And God called the expanse Heaven.[3] And there was evening and there was morning, the second day.

9 And God said, "Let the waters under the heavens be gathered together into one place, and let the dry land appear." And it was so. **10** God called the dry land Earth,[4] and the waters that were gathered together he called Seas. And God saw that it was good.

11 And God said, "Let the earth sprout vegetation, plants[5] yielding seed, and fruit trees bearing fruit in which is their seed, each according to its kind, on the

1. Or *a canopy*; also verses 7, 8, 14, 15, 17, 20.
2. Or *fashioned*; also verse 16.
3. Or *Sky*; also verses 9, 14, 15, 17, 20, 26, 28, 30; 2:1.
4. Or *Land*; also verses 11, 12, 22, 24, 25, 26, 28, 30; 2:1.
5. Or *small plants*; also verses 12, 29.

earth." And it was so. ¹² The earth brought forth vegetation, plants yielding seed according to their own kinds, and trees bearing fruit in which is their seed, each according to its kind. And God saw that it was good. ¹³ And there was evening and there was morning, the third day.

¹⁴ And God said, "Let there be lights in the expanse of the heavens to separate the day from the night. And let them be for signs and for seasons,⁶ and for days and years, ¹⁵ and let them be lights in the expanse of the heavens to give light upon the earth." And it was so. ¹⁶ And God made the two great lights — the greater light to rule the day and the lesser light to rule the night — and the stars. ¹⁷ And God set them in the expanse of the heavens to give light on the earth, ¹⁸ to rule over the day and over the night, and to separate the light from the darkness. And God saw that it was good. ¹⁹ And there was evening and there was morning, the fourth day.

²⁰ And God said, "Let the waters swarm with swarms of living creatures, and let birds⁷ fly above the earth across the expanse of the heavens." ²¹ So God created the great sea creatures and every living creature that moves, with which the waters swarm, according to their kinds, and every winged bird according to its kind. And God saw that it was good. ²² And God blessed them, saying, "Be fruitful and multiply and fill the waters in the seas, and let birds multiply on the earth." ²³ And there was evening and there was morning, the fifth day.

²⁴ And God said, "Let the earth bring forth living creatures according to their kinds — livestock and

What does it mean "creation was good"?

6. Or *appointed times.*
7. Or *flying things;* see Leviticus 11:19–20.

creeping things and beasts of the earth according to their kinds." And it was so. 25 And God made the beasts of the earth according to their kinds and the livestock according to their kinds, and everything that creeps on the ground according to its kind. And God saw that it was good.

26 Then God said, "Let us make man[8] in our image, after our likeness. And let them have dominion over the fish of the sea and over the birds of the heavens and over the livestock and over all the earth and over every creeping thing that creeps on the earth."

27 So God created man in his own image,
in the image of God he created him;
male and female he created them.

28 And God blessed them. And God said to them, "Be fruitful and multiply and fill the earth and subdue it, and have dominion over the fish of the sea and over the birds of the heavens and over every living thing that moves on the earth." 29 And God said, "Behold, I have given you every plant yielding seed that is on the face of all the earth, and every tree with seed in its fruit. You shall have them for food. 30 And to every beast of the earth and to every bird of the heavens and to everything that creeps on the earth, everything that has the breath of life, I have given every green plant for food." And it was so. 31 And God saw everything that he had made, and behold, it was very good. And there was evening and there was morning, the sixth day.

FACT

And there was evening and there was morning — a literal 24-hour day.

---

8. The Hebrew word for *man* (*adam*) is the generic term for mankind and becomes the proper name *Adam*.

What does it mean to you to know you have a Creator who loves you enough to die for you? (John 15:13 and Romans 5:8).

The moon and stars to rule over the night, for his steadfast love endures forever.
Psalm 136:9

cross-ref

The Seventh Day, God Rests

2 Thus the heavens and the earth were finished, and all the host of them. **2** And on the seventh day God finished his work that he had done, and he rested on the seventh day from all his work that he had done. **3** So God blessed the seventh day and made it holy, because on it God rested from all his work that he had done in creation.

Most of Genesis 2 is focusing on events of day 6 of creation.

FACT

The Creation of Man and Woman

4 These are the generations of the heavens and the earth when they were created,
in the day that the LORD God made the earth and the heavens.

5 When no bush of the field[1] was yet in the land[2] and no small plant of the field had yet sprung up — for the LORD God had not caused it to rain on the land, and there was no man to work the ground, **6** and a mist[3] was going up from the land and was watering the whole face of the ground — **7** then the LORD God formed the man of dust from the ground and breathed into his nostrils the breath of life, and the man became a living creature. **8** And the LORD God planted a garden in Eden, in the east, and there he put the man whom he had formed. **9** And out of the ground the LORD God made to spring up every tree that is pleasant to the sight and good for food. The tree of life was in the midst of the garden, and the tree of the knowledge of good and evil.

1. Or *open country.*
2. Or *earth;* also verse 6.
3. Or *spring.*

10 A river flowed out of Eden to water the garden, and there it divided and became four rivers. **11** The name of the first is the Pishon. It is the one that flowed around the whole land of Havilah, where there is gold. **12** And the gold of that land is good; bdellium and onyx stone are there. **13** The name of the second river is the Gihon. It is the one that flowed around the whole land of Cush. **14** And the name of the third river is the Tigris, which flows east of Assyria. And the fourth river is the Euphrates.

15 The LORD God took the man and put him in the garden of Eden to work it and keep it. **16** And the LORD God commanded the man, saying, "You may surely eat of every tree of the garden, **17** but of the tree of the knowledge of good and evil you shall not eat, for in the day that you eat⁴ of it you shall surely die."

18 Then the LORD God said, "It is not good that the man should be alone; I will make him a helper fit for⁵ him." **19** Now out of the ground the LORD God had formed⁶ every beast of the field and every bird of the heavens and brought them to the man to see what he would call them. And whatever the man called every living creature, that was its name. **20** The man gave names to all livestock and to the birds of the heavens and to every beast of the field. But for Adam⁷ there was not found a helper fit for him. **21** So the LORD God caused a deep sleep to fall upon the man, and while he slept took one of his ribs and closed up its place with flesh. **22** And the rib that the

Did you know ribs regenerate? Adam's missing rib would have grown back!

---

4. Or *when you eat*
5. Or *corresponding to;* also verse 20.
6. Or *And out of the ground the LORD God formed.*
7. Or *the man.*

Lord God had taken from the man he made[8] into a woman and brought her to the man. **23** Then the man said,

> "This at last is bone of my bones
> and flesh of my flesh;
> she shall be called Woman,
> because she was taken out of Man."[9]

24 Therefore a man shall leave his father and his mother and hold fast to his wife, and they shall become one flesh. **25** And the man and his wife were both naked and were not ashamed.

FACT

God made a man and a woman — the basis for marriage.

---

8. Hebrew *built*.
9. The Hebrew words for *woman* (*ishshah*) and *man* (*ish*) sound alike.

Did you notice how God has been involved closely with His creation — especially Adam and Eve? How is this different from the "distant and unknowable god" the media often portrays?

_____

_____

_____

_____

_____

_____

_____

_____

_____

_____

_____

_____

_____

_____

For Adam was formed first, then Eve (1 Timothy 2:13).

_____

_____

_____

_____

_____

The Fall

3 Now the serpent was more crafty than any other beast of the field that the Lord God had made. He said to the woman, "Did God actually say, 'You[1] shall not eat of any tree in the garden'?" [2] And the woman said to the serpent, "We may eat of the fruit of the trees in the garden, [3] but God said, 'You shall not eat of the fruit of the tree that is in the midst of the garden, neither shall you touch it, lest you die.' " [4] But the serpent said to the woman, "You will not surely die. [5] For God knows that when you eat of it your eyes will be opened, and you will be like God, knowing good and evil." [6] So when the woman saw that the tree was good for food, and that it was a delight to the eyes, and that the tree was to be desired to make one wise,[2] she took of its fruit and ate, and she also gave some to her husband who was with her, and he ate. [7] Then the eyes of both were opened, and they knew that they were naked. And they sewed fig leaves together and made themselves loincloths.

[8] And they heard the sound of the Lord God walking in the garden in the cool[3] of the day, and the man and his wife hid themselves from the presence of the Lord God among the trees of the garden. [9] But the Lord God called to the man and said to him, "Where are you?"[4] [10] And he said, "I heard the sound of you in the garden, and I was afraid, because I was naked, and I hid myself." [11] He said, "Who told you that you were

FACT

Do animals talk? Parrots do! But they don't make sense. Satan's influence on the serpent caused it to make sense.

---

1. In Hebrew *you* is plural in verses 1–5.
2. Or *to give insight*.
3. Hebrew *wind*.
4. In Hebrew *you* is singular in verses 9 and 11.

naked? Have you eaten of the tree of which I commanded you not to eat?" **12** The man said, "The woman
whom you gave to be with me, she gave me fruit of the
tree, and I ate." **13** Then the Lᴏʀᴅ God said to the
woman, "What is this that you have done?" The woman
said, "The serpent deceived me, and I ate."

14 The Lᴏʀᴅ God said to the serpent,

> "Because you have done this,
> cursed are you above all livestock
> and above all beasts of the field;
> on your belly you shall go,
> and dust you shall eat
> all the days of your life.
> **15** I will put enmity between you and the
> woman,
> and between your offspring[5] and her off-
> spring;
> he shall bruise your head,
> and you shall bruise his heel."

16 To the woman he said,

> "I will surely multiply your pain in
> childbearing;
> in pain you shall bring forth
> children.
> Your desire shall be for[6] your husband, and he
> shall rule over you."

Did you realize that sin caused the world to be full of death and suffering?

17 And to Adam he said,

> "Because you have listened to the voice of
> your wife

---

5. Hebrew *seed*; so throughout Genesis.
6. Or *against*.

and have eaten of the tree
of which I commanded you,
'You shall not eat of it,'
cursed is the ground because of you;
in pain you shall eat of it all the days of your
life;
18 thorns and thistles it shall bring forth for
you;
and you shall eat the plants of the field.
19 By the sweat of your face
you shall eat bread,
till you return to the ground,
for out of it you were taken;
for you are dust,
and to dust you shall return."

20 The man called his wife's name Eve, because she was the mother of all living.[7] 21 And the Lord God made for Adam and for his wife garments of skins and clothed them.

22 Then the Lord God said, "Behold, the man has become like one of us in knowing good and evil. Now, lest he reach out his hand and take also of the tree of life and eat, and live forever —" 23 therefore the Lord God sent him out from the garden of Eden to work the ground from which he was taken. 24 He drove out the man, and at the east of the garden of Eden he placed the cherubim and a flaming sword that turned every way to guard the way to the tree of life.

cross-ref

And the soldiers twisted together a crown of thorns and put it on his head (John 19:2a). But if it bears thorns and thistles, it is worthless and near to being cursed, and its end is to be burned (Hebrews 6:8).

---

7.   *Eve* sounds like the Hebrew for *life-giver* and resembles the word for *living*.

When we see people suffer and die tragically, we often ask, "Why did God make the world this way?" But when you realize that it was due to man's sin and God came to rescue us from sin (and death), how does that make you feel?

_____

_____

_____

_____

_____

_____

_____

_____

_____

_____

_____

_____

_____

Romans 5:12

See page 160

_____

_____

_____

_____

_____

_____

Cain and Abel

4 Now Adam knew Eve his wife, and she conceived and bore Cain, saying, "I have gotten[1] a man with the help of the LORD." **2** And again, she bore his brother Abel. Now Abel was a keeper of sheep, and Cain a worker of the ground. **3** In the course of time Cain brought to the LORD an offering of the fruit of the ground, **4** and Abel also brought of the first-born of his flock and of their fat portions. And the LORD had regard for Abel and his offering, **5** but for Cain and his offering he had no regard. So Cain was very angry, and his face fell. **6** The LORD said to Cain, "Why are you angry, and why has your face fallen? **7** If you do well, will you not be accepted?[2] And if you do not do well, sin is crouching at the door. Its desire is for[3] you, but you must rule over it." **8** Cain spoke to Abel his brother.[4] And when they were in the field, Cain rose up against his brother Abel and killed him. **9** Then the LORD said to Cain, "Where is Abel your brother?" He said, "I do not know; am I my brother's keeper?" **10** And the LORD said, "What have you done? The voice of your brother's blood is crying to me from the ground. **11** And now you are cursed from the ground, which has opened its mouth to receive your brother's blood from your hand. **12** When you work the ground, it shall no longer yield to you its strength. You shall be a fugitive and a wanderer on the earth." **13** Cain said to the LORD,

FACT

The punishment for sin is death (Genesis 2:17, 3:21) and Abel properly offered fat portions, doing the right thing (1 John 3:12).

---

1. Cain sounds like the Hebrew for gotten.
2. Hebrew will there not be a lifting up [of your face]?
3. Or against.
4. Hebrew; Samaritan, Septuagint, Syriac, Vulgate add Let us go out to the field.

"My punishment is greater than I can bear.[5] 14 Behold, you have driven me today away from the ground, and from your face I shall be hidden. I shall be a fugitive and a wanderer on the earth, and whoever finds me will kill me." 15 Then the LORD said to him, "Not so! If anyone kills Cain, vengeance shall be taken on him sevenfold." And the LORD put a mark on Cain, lest any who found him should attack him. 16 Then Cain went away from the presence of the LORD and settled in the land of Nod,[6] east of Eden.

17 Cain knew his wife, and she conceived and bore Enoch. When he built a city, he called the name of the city after the name of his son, Enoch. 18 To Enoch was born Irad, and Irad fathered Mehujael, and Mehujael fathered Methushael, and Methushael fathered Lamech. 19 And Lamech took two wives. The name of the one was Adah, and the name of the other Zillah. 20 Adah bore Jabal; he was the father of those who dwell in tents and have livestock. 21 His brother's name was Jubal; he was the father of all those who play the lyre and pipe. 22 Zillah also bore Tubal-cain; he was the forger of all instruments of bronze and iron. The sister of Tubal-cain was Naamah.

Did you know that "Nod" means "land of wandering" — not a place with other people?

23 Lamech said to his wives:

"Adah and Zillah, hear my voice;
you wives of Lamech, listen to what I say:
I have killed a man for wounding me,
a young man for striking me.

5. Or *My guilt is too great to bear.*
6. *Nod* means *wandering.*

24 If Cain's revenge is sevenfold,
then Lamech's is seventy-sevenfold."

25 And Adam knew his wife again, and she bore a son and called his name Seth, for she said, "God has appointed[7] for me another offspring instead of Abel, for Cain killed him." 26 To Seth also a son was born, and he called his name Enosh. At that time people began to call upon the name of the LORD.

FACT

Cain's wife would have been his sister! This was not forbidden until Leviticus 18, in the time of Moses.

---

7. *Seth* sounds like the Hebrew for *he appointed*.

Did you realize that people have always been smart? Tubal-Cain was making things from bronze and iron. How does your view of other people change when you realize that people didn't evolve from unintelligent, brute, evolutionary ancestors?

And he made from one man every nation of mankind to live on all the face of the earth, having determined allotted periods and the boundaries of their dwelling place (Acts 17:26).

Adam's Descendants to Noah

5 This is the book of the generations of Adam. When God created man, he made him in the likeness of God. ² Male and female he created them, and he blessed them and named them Man[1] when they were created. ³ When Adam had lived 130 years, he fathered a son in his own likeness, after his image, and named him Seth. ⁴ The days of Adam after he fathered Seth were 800 years; and he had other sons and daughters. ⁵ Thus all the days that Adam lived were 930 years, and he died.⁶ When Seth had lived 105 years, he fathered Enosh. ⁷ Seth lived after he fathered Enosh 807 years and had other sons and daughters. ⁸ Thus all the days of Seth were 912 years, and he died.

⁹ When Enosh had lived 90 years, he fathered Kenan. ¹⁰ Enosh lived after he fathered Kenan 815 years and had other sons and daughters. ¹¹ Thus all the days of Enosh were 905 years, and he died.

¹² When Kenan had lived 70 years, he fathered Mahalalel. ¹³ Kenan lived after he fathered Mahalalel 840 years and had other sons and daughters. ¹⁴ Thus all the days of Kenan were 910 years, and he died.

¹⁵ When Mahalalel had lived 65 years, he fathered Jared. ¹⁶ Mahalalel lived after he fathered Jared 830 years and had other sons and daughters. ¹⁷ Thus all the days of Mahalalel were 895 years, and he died.

¹⁸ When Jared had lived 162 years he fathered Enoch. ¹⁹ Jared lived after he fathered Enoch 800 years

FACT

Adam talked to Methuselah and Methuselah could have shared this history with Noah!

---

1. Hebrew *adam*.

and had other sons and daughters. **20** Thus all the days of Jared were 962 years, and he died.

21 When Enoch had lived 65 years, he fathered Methuselah. **22** Enoch walked with God[2] after he fathered Methuselah 300 years and had other sons and daughters. **23** Thus all the days of Enoch were 365 years. **24** Enoch walked with God, and he was not,[3] for God took him.

25 When Methuselah had lived 187 years, he fathered Lamech. **26** Methuselah lived after he fathered Lamech 782 years and had other sons and daughters. **27** Thus all the days of Methuselah were 969 years, and he died.

28 When Lamech had lived 182 years, he fathered a son **29** and called his name Noah, saying, "Out of the ground that the Lord has cursed, this one shall bring us relief[4] from our work and from the painful toil of our hands." **30** Lamech lived after he fathered Noah 595 years and had other sons and daughters. **31** Thus all the days of Lamech were 777 years, and he died.

32 After Noah was 500 years old, Noah fathered Shem, Ham, and Japheth.

Did you know that Enoch did not die, but was taken directly without death? (Hebrews 11:5).

---

2. Septuagint *pleased God.*
3. Septuagint *was not found.*
4. *Noah* sounds like the Hebrew for *rest.*

Increasing Corruption on Earth

6 When man began to multiply on the face of the land and daughters were born to them, ²the sons of God saw that the daughters of man were attractive. And they took as their wives any they chose. ³Then the LORD said, "My Spirit shall not abide in¹ man forever, for he is flesh: his days shall be 120 years." ⁴The Nephilim² were on the earth in those days, and also afterward, when the sons of God came in to the daughters of man and they bore children to them. These were the mighty men who were of old, the men of renown.⁵The LORD saw that the wickedness of man was great in the earth, and that every intention of the thoughts of his heart was only evil continually. ⁶And the LORD regretted that he had made man on the earth, and it grieved him to his heart. ⁷So the LORD said, "I will blot out man whom I have created from the face of the land, man and animals and creeping things and birds of the heavens, for I am sorry that I have made them." ⁸But Noah found favor in the eyes of the LORD.

> **FACT**
>
> One hundred twenty years was a countdown to the Flood, not longevity of life. Many people surpassed 120 years.

Noah and the Flood

⁹These are the generations of Noah. Noah was a righteous man, blameless in his generation. Noah walked with God. ¹⁰And Noah had three sons, Shem, Ham, and Japheth.

---

1. Or *My Spirit shall not contend with.*
2. Or *giants.*

11 Now the earth was corrupt in God's sight, and the earth was filled with violence. **12** And God saw the earth, and behold, it was corrupt, for all flesh had corrupted their way on the earth. **13** And God said to Noah, "I have determined to make an end of all flesh,[3] for the earth is filled with violence through them. Behold, I will destroy them with the earth. **14** Make yourself an ark of gopher wood.[4] Make rooms in the ark, and cover it inside and out with pitch. **15** This is how you are to make it: the length of the ark 300 cubits,[5] its breadth 50 cubits, and its height 30 cubits. **16** Make a roof[6]   for the ark, and finish it to a cubit above, and set the door of the ark in its side. Make it with lower, second, and third decks. **17** For behold, I will bring a flood of waters upon the earth to destroy all flesh in which is the breath of life under heaven. Everything that is on the earth shall die. **18** But I will establish my covenant with you, and you shall come into the ark, you, your sons, your wife, and your sons' wives with you. **19** And of every living thing of all flesh, you shall bring two of every sort into the ark to keep them alive with you. They shall be male and female. **20** Of the birds according to their kinds, and of the animals according to their kinds, of every creeping thing of the ground, according to its kind, two of every sort shall come in to you to keep them alive. **21** Also take with you every sort of food that is eaten, and store it up. It shall serve as food for you and for them." **22** Noah did this; he did all that God commanded him.

> Did you know the ark was big enough to hold the required animal kinds (not species, which is not necessarily the same thing).

---

3. Hebrew *The end of all flesh has come before me.*
4. An unknown kind of tree; transliterated from Hebrew.
5. A *cubit* was about 18 inches or 45 centimeters.
6. Or *skylight.*

7 Then the LORD said to Noah, "Go into the ark, you and all your household, for I have seen that you are righteous before me in this generation. ² Take with you seven pairs of all clean animals,¹ the male and his mate, and a pair of the animals that are not clean, the male and his mate, ³ and seven pairs² of the birds of the heavens also, male and female, to keep their offspring alive on the face of all the earth. ⁴ For in seven days I will send rain on the earth forty days and forty nights, and every living thing³ that I have made I will blot out from the face of the ground." ⁵ And Noah did all that the LORD had commanded him. ⁶ Noah was six hundred years old when the flood of waters came upon the earth. ⁷ And Noah and his sons and his wife and his sons' wives with him went into the ark to escape the waters of the flood. ⁸ Of clean animals, and of animals that are not clean, and of birds, and of everything that creeps on the ground, ⁹ two and two, male and female, went into the ark with Noah, as God had commanded Noah. ¹⁰ And after seven days the waters of the flood came upon the earth.

¹¹ In the six hundredth year of Noah's life, in the second month, on the seventeenth day of the month, on that day all the fountains of the great deep burst forth, and the windows of the heavens were opened. ¹² And rain fell upon the earth forty days and forty nights. ¹³ On the very same day Noah and his sons, Shem and Ham and Japheth, and Noah's wife and the three wives of his sons with them entered the ark, ¹⁴ they and every

FACT

Noah was a righteous man, but was likely in tears when the door of the ark shut; remember, he had siblings who died in the Flood.

---

1. Or *seven of each kind of clean animal*.
2. Or *seven of each kind*.
3. Hebrew *all existence*; also verse 23.

beast, according to its kind, and all the livestock according to their kinds, and every creeping thing that creeps on the earth, according to its kind, and every bird, according to its kind, every winged creature. **15** They went into the ark with Noah, two and two of all flesh in which there was the breath of life. **16** And those that entered, male and female of all flesh, went in as God had commanded him. And the LORD shut him in.

17 The flood continued forty days on the earth. The waters increased and bore up the ark, and it rose high above the earth. **18** The waters prevailed and increased greatly on the earth, and the ark floated on the face of the waters. **19** And the waters prevailed so mightily on the earth that all the high mountains under the whole heaven were covered. **20** The waters prevailed above the mountains, covering them fifteen cubits⁴ deep. **21** And all flesh died that moved on the earth, birds, livestock, beasts, all swarming creatures that swarm on the earth, and all mankind. **22** Everything on the dry land in whose nostrils was the breath of life died. **23** He blotted out every living thing that was on the face of the ground, man and animals and creeping things and birds of the heavens. They were blotted out from the earth. Only Noah was left, and those who were with him in the ark. **24** And the waters prevailed on the earth 150 days.

Did you know that verse 19 disproves the idea of a local flood in the Middle East?

---

4.   A *cubit* was about 18 inches or 45 centimeters.

The Flood Subsides

8 But God remembered Noah and all the beasts and all the livestock that were with him in the ark. And God made a wind blow over the earth, and the waters subsided. ² The fountains of the deep and the windows of the heavens were closed, the rain from the heavens was restrained, ³ and the waters receded from the earth continually. At the end of 150 days the waters had abated, ⁴ and in the seventh month, on the seventeenth day of the month, the ark came to rest on the mountains of Ararat. ⁵ And the waters continued to abate until the tenth month; in the tenth month, on the first day of the month, the tops of the mountains were seen. ⁶ At the end of forty days Noah opened the window of the ark that he had made ⁷ and sent forth a raven. It went to and fro until the waters were dried up from the earth. ⁸ Then he sent forth a dove from him, to see if the waters had subsided from the face of the ground. ⁹ But the dove found no place to set her foot, and she returned to him to the ark, for the waters were still on the face of the whole earth. So he put out his hand and took her and brought her into the ark with him. ¹⁰ He waited another seven days, and again he sent forth the dove out of the ark. ¹¹ And the dove came back to him in the evening, and behold, in her mouth was a freshly plucked olive leaf. So Noah knew that the waters had subsided from the earth. ¹² Then he waited another seven days and sent forth the dove, and she did not return to him anymore.

¹³ In the six hundred and first year, in the first month, the first day of the month, the waters were dried from off

> **cross-ref**
>
> The mountains rose; the valleys sank. . . . You set a boundary that they may not pass over, so that they will not return to cover the earth (Psalm 104:8–9; NASB).

the earth. And Noah removed the covering of the ark and looked, and behold, the face of the ground was dry. [14] In the second month, on the twenty-seventh day of the month, the earth had dried out. [15] Then God said to Noah, [16] "Go out from the ark, you and your wife, and your sons and your sons' wives with you. [17] Bring out with you every living thing that is with you of all flesh — birds and animals and every creeping thing that creeps on the earth — that they may swarm on the earth, and be fruitful and multiply on the earth." [18] So Noah went out, and his sons and his wife and his sons' wives with him. [19] Every beast, every creeping thing, and every bird, everything that moves on the earth, went out by families from the ark.

God's Covenant with Noah

[20] Then Noah built an altar to the LORD and took some of every clean animal and some of every clean bird and offered burnt offerings on the altar. [21] And when the LORD smelled the pleasing aroma, the LORD said in his heart, "I will never again curse[1] the ground because of man, for the intention of man's heart is evil from his youth. Neither will I ever again strike down every living creature as I have done. [22] While the earth remains, seedtime and harvest, cold and heat, summer and winter, day and night, shall not cease."

Did you realize that most of the rock layers that contain fossils were from the Flood, not millions of years of slow processes?

---

1. Or *dishonor*.

9 And God blessed Noah and his sons and said to them, "Be fruitful and multiply and fill the earth. 2 The fear of you and the dread of you shall be upon every beast of the earth and upon every bird of the heavens, upon everything that creeps on the ground and all the fish of the sea. Into your hand they are delivered. 3 Every moving thing that lives shall be food for you. And as I gave you the green plants, I give you everything. 4 But you shall not eat flesh with its life, that is, its blood. 5 And for your lifeblood I will require a reckoning: from every beast I will require it and from man. From his fellow man I will require a reckoning for the life of man. 6 "Whoever sheds the blood of man,

by man shall his blood be shed,

for God made man in his own image.

7 And you,[1] be fruitful and multiply, increase greatly on the earth and multiply in it."

8 Then God said to Noah and to his sons with him, 9 "Behold, I establish my covenant with you and your offspring after you, 10 and with every living creature that is with you, the birds, the livestock, and every beast of the earth with you, as many as came out of the ark; it is for every beast of the earth. 11 I establish my covenant with you, that never again shall all flesh be cut off by the waters of the flood, and never again shall there be a flood to destroy the earth." 12 And God said, "This is the sign of the covenant that I make between me and you and every living creature that is with you, for all future generations: 13 I have set my bow in the

FACT

Genesis 9:3 is when God first permitted man to eat meat; before this, man was told to eat a vegetarian diet (Genesis 1:29).

1. In Hebrew you is plural.

cloud, and it shall be a sign of the covenant between me and the earth. **14** When I bring clouds over the earth and the bow is seen in the clouds, **15** I will remember my covenant that is between me and you and every living creature of all flesh. And the waters shall never again become a flood to destroy all flesh. **16** When the bow is in the clouds, I will see it and remember the everlasting covenant between God and every living creature of all flesh that is on the earth." **17** God said to Noah, "This is the sign of the covenant that I have established between me and all flesh that is on the earth."

Noah's Descendants

18 The sons of Noah who went forth from the ark were Shem, Ham, and Japheth. (Ham was the father of Canaan.) **19** These three were the sons of Noah, and from these the people of the whole earth were dispersed.²

20 Noah began to be a man of the soil, and he planted a vineyard.³ **21** He drank of the wine and became drunk and lay uncovered in his tent. **22** And Ham, the father of Canaan, saw the nakedness of his father and told his two brothers outside. **23** Then Shem and Japheth took a garment, laid it on both their shoulders, and walked backward and covered the nakedness of their father. Their faces were turned backward, and they did not see their father's nakedness. **24** When Noah awoke from his wine and knew what his youngest son had done to him, **25** he said,

> Did you know that the rainbow promise is further proof of a global Flood? We see local floods all the time!

---

2. Or *from these the whole earth was populated.*
3. Or *Noah, a man of the soil, was the first to plant a vineyard.*

"Cursed be Canaan;
a servant of servants shall he be to his brothers."

26 He also said,

Blessed be the LORD, the God of Shem;
and let Canaan be his servant.
27 May God enlarge Japheth,[4]
and let him dwell in the tents of Shem,
and let Canaan be his servant."

28 After the flood Noah lived 350 years.
29 All the days of Noah were 950 years, and he died.

FACT

Noah knew better than to curse Ham, whom God had blessed. So he cursed Canaan, who was like Ham but worse. Many of Canaan's descendents turned out to be very bad.

---

4. *Japheth* sounds like the Hebrew for *enlarge*.

Did you realize the Flood was a judgment on sin and yet God sent a means of salvation with the ark? Did you notice how Christ is the means of salvation for the final judgment?

For they deliberately overlook this fact, that the heavens existed long ago, and the earth was formed out of water and through water by the word of God, and that by means of these the world that then existed was deluged with water and perished. But by the same word the heavens and earth that now exist are stored up for fire, being kept until the day of judgment and destruction of the ungodly (2 Peter 3:5–7).

Nations Descended From Noah

10 These are the generations of the sons of Noah, Shem, Ham, and Japheth. Sons were born to them after the flood. [2] The sons of Japheth: Gomer, Magog, Madai, Javan, Tubal, Meshech, and Tiras. [3] The sons of Gomer: Ashkenaz, Riphath, and Togarmah. [4] The sons of Javan: Elishah, Tarshish, Kittim, and Dodanim. [5] From these the coastland peoples spread in their lands, each with his own language, by their clans, in their nations.

[6] The sons of Ham: Cush, Egypt, Put, and Canaan. [7] The sons of Cush: Seba, Havilah, Sabtah, Raamah, and Sabteca. The sons of Raamah: Sheba and Dedan. [8] Cush fathered Nimrod; he was the first on earth to be a mighty man.[1] [9] He was a mighty hunter before the Lord. Therefore it is said, "Like Nimrod a mighty hunter before the Lord." [10] The beginning of his kingdom was Babel, Erech, Accad, and Calneh, in the land of Shinar. [11] From that land he went into Assyria and built Nineveh, Rehoboth-Ir, Calah, and [12] Resen between Nineveh and Calah; that is the great city. [13] Egypt fathered Ludim, Anamim, Lehabim, Naphtuhim, [14] Pathrusim, Casluhim (from whom[2] the Philistines came), and Caphtorim.

[15] Canaan fathered Sidon his firstborn and Heth, [16] and the Jebusites, the Amorites, the Girgashites, [17] the Hivites, the Arkites, the Sinites, [18] the Arvadites, the Zemarites, and the Hamathites. Afterward the clans of the Canaanites dispersed. [19] And the territory of the

> **FACT**
>
> **These genealogies are actually a breakdown of what occurs in Genesis 11:1–9, which is the chronological account.**

---

1. Or *he began to be a mighty man on the earth.*
2. Or *from where.*

Canaanites extended from Sidon in the direction of Gerar as far as Gaza, and in the direction of Sodom, Gomorrah, Admah, and Zeboiim, as far as Lasha. 20 These are the sons of Ham, by their clans, their languages, their lands, and their nations.

21 To Shem also, the father of all the children of Eber, the elder brother of Japheth, children were born. 22 The sons of Shem: Elam, Asshur, Arpachshad, Lud, and Aram. 23 The sons of Aram: Uz, Hul, Gether, and Mash. 24 Arpachshad fathered Shelah; and Shelah fathered Eber. 25 To Eber were born two sons: the name of the one was Peleg,[3] for in his days the earth was divided, and his brother's name was Joktan. 26 Joktan fathered Almodad, Sheleph, Hazarmaveth, Jerah, 27 Hadoram, Uzal, Diklah, 28 Obal, Abimael, Sheba, 29 Ophir, Havilah, and Jobab; all these were the sons of Joktan. 30 The territory in which they lived extended from Mesha in the direction of Sephar to the hill country of the east. 31 These are the sons of Shem, by their clans, their languages, their lands, and their nations.

32 These are the clans of the sons of Noah, according to their genealogies, in their nations, and from these the nations spread abroad on the earth after the flood.

> **Did you know that Cush is Ethiopia, Javan is Greece, and Elam is Persia (Iran)? These names pop up in all sorts of cultures all over the globe!**

---

3. *Peleg* means *division*.

The Tower of Babel

11 Now the whole earth had one language and the same words. ² And as people migrated from the east, they found a plain in the land of Shinar and settled there. ³ And they said to one another, "Come, let us make bricks, and burn them thoroughly." And they had brick for stone, and bitumen for mortar. ⁴ Then they said, "Come, let us build ourselves a city and a tower with its top in the heavens, and let us make a name for ourselves, lest we be dispersed over the face of the whole earth." ⁵ And the LORD came down to see the city and the tower, which the children of man had built. ⁶ And the LORD said, "Behold, they are one people, and they have all one language, and this is only the beginning of what they will do. And nothing that they propose to do will now be impossible for them. ⁷ Come, let us go down and there confuse their language, so that they may not understand one another's speech." ⁸ So the LORD dispersed them from there over the face of all the earth, and they left off building the city. ⁹ Therefore its name was called Babel, because there the LORD confused¹ the language of all the earth. And from there the LORD dispersed them over the face of all the earth.

FACT

People were defying God's command to be fruitful, multiply, and fill the earth in Genesis 9:1.

Shem's Descendants

¹⁰ These are the generations of Shem. When Shem was 100 years old, he fathered Arpachshad two years after the flood. ¹¹ And Shem lived after he fathered Arpachshad 500 years and had other sons and daughters.

1. *Babel* sounds like the Hebrew for *confused*.

¹²When Arpachshad had lived 35 years, he fathered Shelah. ¹³ And Arpachshad lived after he fathered Shelah 403 years and had other sons and daughters.

¹⁴ When Shelah had lived 30 years, he fathered Eber. ¹⁵ And Shelah lived after he fathered Eber 403 years and had other sons and daughters.

¹⁶ When Eber had lived 34 years, he fathered Peleg. ¹⁷ And Eber lived after he fathered Peleg 430 years and had other sons and daughters.

¹⁸ When Peleg had lived 30 years, he fathered Reu. ¹⁹ And Peleg lived after he fathered Reu 209 years and had other sons and daughters.

²⁰ When Reu had lived 32 years, he fathered Serug. ²¹ And Reu lived after he fathered Serug 207 years and had other sons and daughters.

²² When Serug had lived 30 years, he fathered Nahor. ²³ And Serug lived after he fathered Nahor 200 years and had other sons and daughters.

²⁴ When Nahor had lived 29 years, he fathered Terah. ²⁵ And Nahor lived after he fathered Terah 119 years and had other sons and daughters.

²⁶ When Terah had lived 70 years, he fathered Abram, Nahor, and Haran.

> **Did you know the Tower was built, but the city is what they stopped building?**
> **(Genesis 11:5 and 11:8.)**

Terah's Descendants

²⁷ Now these are the generations of Terah. Terah fathered Abram, Nahor, and Haran; and Haran fathered Lot. ²⁸ Haran died in the presence of his father Terah in the land of his kindred, in Ur of the Chaldeans. ²⁹ And Abram and Nahor took wives. The name of Abram's wife was Sarai, and the name of Nahor's wife,

Milcah, the daughter of Haran the father of Milcah and Iscah. 30 Now Sarai was barren; she had no child.

31 Terah took Abram his son and Lot the son of Haran, his grandson, and Sarai his daughter-in-law, his son Abram's wife, and they went forth together from Ur of the Chaldeans to go into the land of Canaan, but when they came to Haran, they settled there. 32 The days of Terah were 205 years, and Terah died in Haran.

FACT

Abraham was a Hebrew (Genesis 14:13), meaning he came from the tribe of Eber, his ancestor at the Tower of Babel (Genesis 11:16).

There are parallels between the historical account of Noah's ark and Jesus as the "ark" or means of salvation in the New Testament. People hear the truth and either receive Jesus, or reject salvation. Those on the ark had to have family that rejected the truth, despite Noah telling the people for perhaps 55 to 75 years[1] during the ark's construction of the judgment to come. How has your life changed since you received Christ and how has this impacted your relationship with those who may have not yet had the chance for salvation? Do you share your salvation with family and friends?

Biblical genealogies (Genesis 10 and 11:10–26, for example) provide not only a chronological time-line, but also history for many early cultures.

1. www.answersingenesis.org/articles/2010/06/01/long-to-build-the-ark.

A Brief Review of History from Abram to Moses and the Ten Commandments

After this, the Bible picks up with the call of Abram, who was later named Abraham (Genesis 17:5[1]). He and his wife, Sarah, had a son named Isaac. The Lord made a promise that Abraham's descendants would inherit the Promised Land (Genesis 12:7[2]), where the Canaanites were, and were becoming increasingly sinful (Genesis 15:16[3]). Isaac married Rebekah, and they had twins, Esau and Jacob. Esau sold his birthright to Jacob, who really desired it (Genesis 25), and Jacob ultimately received the blessing as well (Genesis 27).

Jacob was renamed Israel (Genesis 32:28[4]) and had 12 sons. One son, Joseph, was sold into slavery in Egypt by his brothers, unknown to their father Jacob (Genesis 37), but Joseph rose in power to become the second most powerful person in Egypt after the pharaoh (Genesis 41:41[5]). During a long drought, people came from all over to buy grain from Egypt, as Joseph had foreseen the drought and prepared for it by the grace of God. Jacob and Joseph's brothers also came to Egypt to buy grain, and ultimately Joseph revealed to his family who he was (Genesis 45).

The Israelites then remained in Egypt and prospered for several hundred years. But a pharaoh came to power who had forgotten about

---

1. No longer shall your name be called Abram, but your name shall be Abraham, for I have made you the father of a multitude of nations.
2. Then the LORD appeared to Abram and said, "To your offspring I will give this land." So he built there an altar to the LORD, who had appeared to him.
3. And they shall come back here in the fourth generation, for the iniquity of the Amorites is not yet complete."
4. Then he said, "Your name shall no longer be called Jacob, but Israel, for you have striven with God and with men, and have prevailed."
5. And Pharaoh said to Joseph, "See, I have set you over all the land of Egypt."

Joseph and all he did for Egypt (Exodus 1:8[6]). This pharaoh made the Israelites slaves (Exodus 1:13[7]) and even killed many young baby boys during his reign (Exodus 1:22[8]). However, one in the pharaoh's own house rescued one boy who was floating in a basket and took him under her wing (Exodus 2:1–10). He grew in the pharaoh's household, and his name was Moses.

This began a series of events between Moses, whom the Lord instructed to free the Israelites, and the pharaoh (Exodus 3). The Lord miraculously called down ten plagues on the Egyptians and the pharaoh until they released the Israelites (Exodus 5–12). Then by another miraculous happening, the Lord used Moses to part the Red Sea and allow the Israelites to escape from the pharaoh (Exodus 14:21–30). Of course, there are many more details, but this leads us up to Moses presenting the Israelites with the Ten Commandments that God gave to him.

---

6. Now there arose a new king over Egypt, who did not know Joseph.
7. So they ruthlessly made the people of Israel work as slaves.
8. Then Pharaoh commanded all his people, "Every son that is born to the Hebrews you shall cast into the Nile, but you shall let every daughter live."

Exodus

The Ten Commandments

20 And God spoke all these words, saying, **2** "I am the LORD your God, who brought you out of the land of Egypt, out of the house of slavery.

3 "You shall have no other gods before[1] me.

4 "You shall not make for yourself a carved image, or any likeness of anything that is in heaven above, or that is in the earth beneath, or that is in the water under the earth. **5** You shall not bow down to them or serve them, for I the LORD your God am a jealous God, visiting the iniquity of the fathers on the children to the third and the fourth generation of those who hate me, **6** but showing steadfast love to thousands[2] of those who love me and keep my commandments.

7 "You shall not take the name of the LORD your God in vain, for the LORD will not hold him guiltless who takes his name in vain.

8 "Remember the Sabbath day, to keep it holy. **9** Six days you shall labor, and do all your work, **10** but the seventh day is a Sabbath to the LORD your God. On it you shall not do any work, you, or your son, or your daughter, your male servant, or your female servant, or your livestock, or the sojourner who is within your gates. **11** For in six days the LORD made heaven and earth, the sea, and all that is in them, and rested on the

FACT

Some people want morality without the Bible, and without God. But without God and the Bible, there is no such thing as right and wrong. People who want morality must borrow from the Bible.

---

1. Or *besides.*
2. Or *to the thousandth generation.*

seventh day. Therefore the LORD blessed the Sabbath day and made it holy.

12 "Honor your father and your mother, that your days may be long in the land that the LORD your God is giving you.

13 "You shall not murder.[3]

14 "You shall not commit adultery.

15 "You shall not steal.

16 "You shall not bear false witness against your neighbor.

17 "You shall not covet your neighbor's house; you shall not covet your neighbor's wife, or his male servant, or his female servant, or his ox, or his donkey, or anything that is your neighbor's."

When asked which was the greatest commandment, Jesus said, "You shall love the Lord your God with all your heart and with all your soul and with all your mind" (Matthew 22:37).

---

3. The Hebrew word also covers causing human death through carelessness or negligence.

A Brief Review of History from the Ten Commandments to Christ

After the Israelites received the Ten Commandments they were disobedient, even after witnessing the awesome power of God in Egypt (the ten plagues, parting of the Red Sea, and so on). They were forced to wander in the wilderness for 40 years until that generation of unbelievers died (Joshua 5:6).[1] Then, being led by Joshua, the Israelites went into the Promised Land to judge the Canaanites (some descendants of Noah's grandson Canaan), whose sin had reached its full measure (Leviticus 18). This was the time of the judges that included Deborah and Samson (a couple of famous judges).

But the Israelites asked for a king (1 Samuel 8:6–7),[2] to be like the other nations (but they were really rejecting God as their king). The Lord in His grace gave them Saul, who reigned for 40 years and did not do a very good job. Then there was David, Saul's son-in-law, who reigned for 40 years and was a king after the Lord's own heart but wasn't perfect. Then Solomon, David's son, ruled for 40 years, and even with the great wisdom that the Lord gave Solomon, he still turned his heart away from God by the end of his life. So the Lord split the kingdom in two: a Northern Kingdom, Israel, with a new kingship and the Southern Kingdom, Judah, which continued with David and Solomon's line.

Each kingdom had various kings, some good, such as Hezekiah, and some bad. The Israelites kept turning from

---

1. Joshua 5:6: For the people of Israel walked forty years in the wilderness, until all the nation, the men of war who came out of Egypt, perished, because they did not obey the voice of the LORD; the LORD swore to them that he would not let them see the land that the LORD had sworn to their fathers to give to us, a land flowing with milk and honey.

2. 1 Samuel 8:6–7: But the thing displeased Samuel when they said, "Give us a king to judge us." And Samuel prayed to the LORD. And the LORD said to Samuel, "Obey the voice of the people in all that they say to you, for they have not rejected you, but they have rejected me from being king over them."

God and His Word. So the Lord kept sending prophets to help bring them back and warn them of what would happen if they didn't. You may have heard the names of some of the famous prophets such as Jeremiah, Elijah, or Isaiah.

Ultimately, the Israelites, who kept falling further and further from God, went into captivity, just as Leviticus 18:24–28[3] had warned. The Northern Kingdom was captured by Assyria (a nation that had arisen from Noah's grandson Asshur) (2 Kings 17:5; 23)[4] and the Southern Kingdom to the Babylonian empire (a kingdom that was centered where Babel used to be and where Nimrod [Noah's great grandson] took over after the event at Babel) (2 Kings 24:15–16).[5] Esther and Daniel were prominent during this time.

Finally, the Israelites were permitted to return. This was the time of Ezra, and one may recall the strife Nehemiah had while trying to rebuild the wall at Jerusalem. Then we have the last three prophets, Haggai, Zechariah, and Malachi. Following that was 400 years of silence from the Lord because the Israelites were still being disobedient.

During this time Alexander the Great conquered the whole area and Greek became one of the popular languages of the day — and the New Testament was written in Greek as a result. Then the Roman Empire conquered the Greeks, and it was the Romans who were in

---

3. Leviticus 18:24–28: Do not make yourselves unclean by any of these things, for by all these the nations I am driving out before you have become unclean, and the land became unclean, so that I punished its iniquity, and the land vomited out its inhabitants. But you shall keep my statutes and my rules and do none of these abominations, either the native or the stranger who sojourns among you (for the people of the land, who were before you, did all of these abominations, so that the land became unclean), lest the land vomit you out when you make it unclean, as it vomited out the nation that was before you.

4. 2 Kings 17:5: Then the king of Assyria invaded all the land and came to Samaria, and for three years he besieged it.
2 Kings 17:23: until the LORD removed Israel out of his sight, as he had spoken by all his servants the prophets. So Israel was exiled from their own land to Assyria until this day.

5. 2 Kings 24:15–16: And he carried away Jehoiachin to Babylon. The king's mother, the king's wives, his officials, and the chief men of the land he took into captivity from Jerusalem to Babylon. And the king of Babylon brought captive to Babylon all the men of valor, 7,000, and the craftsmen and the metal workers, 1,000, all of them strong and fit for war.

control when Jesus Christ was born of a virgin to fulfill Genesis 3:15[6] and Isaiah 7:14[7] as a miraculous entrance into the world (in Bethlehem).

The Romans had a provincial ruler/king in place in Judea (Israel) named Herod, and John the Baptist prepared the way for the Lord Jesus Christ. This brings us to the Gospel. There are four complementary accounts of Jesus' life preserved in Matthew, Mark, Luke, and John. This is the gospel of Jesus Christ, according to John, one of His disciples.

---

6. Genesis 3:15: I will put enmity between you and the woman, and between your offspring and her offspring; he shall bruise your head, and you shall bruise his heel."

7. Isaiah 7:14: Therefore the Lord himself will give you a sign. Behold, the virgin shall conceive and bear a son, and shall call his name Immanuel.

The Gospel According to John

The Word Became Flesh

1 In the beginning was the Word, and the Word was with God, and the Word was God. ² He was in the beginning with God. ³ All things were made through him, and without him was not any thing made that was made. ⁴ In him was life,[1] and the life was the light of men. ⁵ The light shines in the darkness, and the darkness has not overcome it. ⁶ There was a man sent from God, whose name was John. ⁷ He came as a witness, to bear witness about the light, that all might believe through him. ⁸ He was not the light, but came to bear witness about the light.

FACT

The Word (Jesus Christ) is God, not a created entity (Colossians 1; Hebrews 1). He became a man, our relative, to die in our place.

⁹ The true light, which gives light to everyone, was coming into the world. ¹⁰ He was in the world, and the world was made through him, yet the world did not know him. ¹¹ He came to his own,[2] and his own people[3] did not receive him. ¹² But to all who did receive him, who believed in his name, he gave the right to become children of God, ¹³ who were born, not of blood nor of the will of the flesh nor of the will of man, but of God.

¹⁴ And the Word became flesh and dwelt among us, and we have seen his glory, glory as of the only Son from the Father, full of grace and truth. ¹⁵ (John bore witness about him, and cried out, "This was he of whom I said, 'He who comes after me ranks before me,

---

1. Or *was not any thing made. That which has been made was life in him.*
2. Greek *to his own things;* that is, to his own domain, or to his own people.
3. *People* is implied in Greek.

because he was before me.'") **16** For from his fullness we have all received, grace upon grace.[4] **17** For the law was given through Moses; grace and truth came through Jesus Christ. **18** No one has ever seen God; the only God,[5] who is at the Father's side,[6] he has made him known.

The Testimony of John the Baptist

19 And this is the testimony of John, when the Jews sent priests and Levites from Jerusalem to ask him, "Who are you?" **20** He confessed, and did not deny, but confessed, "I am not the Christ." **21** And they asked him, "What then? Are you Elijah?" He said, "I am not." "Are you the Prophet?" And he answered, "No." **22** So they said to him, "Who are you? We need to give an answer to those who sent us. What do you say about yourself?" **23** He said, "I am the voice of one crying out in the wilderness, 'Make straight[7] the way of the Lord,' as the prophet Isaiah said."

24 (Now they had been sent from the Pharisees.) **25** They asked him, "Then why are you baptizing, if you are neither the Christ, nor Elijah, nor the Prophet?" **26** John answered them, "I baptize with water, but among you stands one you do not know, **27** even he who comes after me, the strap of whose sandal I am not worthy to untie." **28** These things took place in Bethany across the Jordan, where John was baptizing.

> **Did you know some cults say Jesus is not God? In doing this, they change John 1, Colossians 1, and Hebrews 1, to their own destruction — their faith is no longer in the Christ of the Bible, but one of their own making.**

---

4. Or *grace in place of grace.*
5. Or *the only One, who is God;* some manuscripts *the only Son.*
6. Greek *in the bosom of the Father.*
7. Or *crying out, 'In the wilderness make straight.*

Behold, the Lamb of God

29 The next day he saw Jesus coming toward him, and said, "Behold, the Lamb of God, who takes away the sin of the world! **30** This is he of whom I said, 'After me comes a man who ranks before me, because he was before me.' **31** I myself did not know him, but for this purpose I came baptizing with water, that he might be revealed to Israel." **32** And John bore witness: "I saw the Spirit descend from heaven like a dove, and it remained on him. **33** I myself did not know him, but he who sent me to baptize with water said to me, 'He on whom you see the Spirit descend and remain, this is he who baptizes with the Holy Spirit.' **34** And I have seen and have borne witness that this is the Son of God."

cross-ref

For Christ, our Passover lamb, has been sacrificed (1 Corinthians 5:7b).
. . . but with the precious blood of Christ, like that of a lamb without blemish or spot (1 Peter 1:19).

Jesus Calls the First Disciples

35 The next day again John was standing with two of his disciples, **36** and he looked at Jesus as he walked by and said, "Behold, the Lamb of God!" **37** The two disciples heard him say this, and they followed Jesus. **38** Jesus turned and saw them following and said to them, "What are you seeking?" And they said to him, "Rabbi" (which means Teacher), "where are you staying?" **39** He said to them, "Come and you will see." So they came and saw where he was staying, and they stayed with him that day, for it was about the tenth hour.[8] **40** One of the two who heard John speak and followed Jesus[9] was Andrew, Simon Peter's brother.

---

8. That is, about 4 P.M.
9. Greek *him.*

41 He first found his own brother Simon and said to him, "We have found the Messiah" (which means Christ). **42** He brought him to Jesus. Jesus looked at him and said, "You are Simon the son of John. You shall be called Cephas" (which means Peter[10]).

Jesus Calls Philip and Nathanael

43 The next day Jesus decided to go to Galilee. He found Philip and said to him, "Follow me." **44** Now Philip was from Bethsaida, the city of Andrew and Peter. **45** Philip found Nathanael and said to him, "We have found him of whom Moses in the Law and also the prophets wrote, Jesus of Nazareth, the son of Joseph." **46** Nathanael said to him, "Can anything good come out of Nazareth?" Philip said to him, "Come and see." **47** Jesus saw Nathanael coming toward him and said of him, "Behold, an Israelite indeed, in whom there is no deceit!" **48** Nathanael said to him, "How do you know me?" Jesus answered him, "Before Philip called you, when you were under the fig tree, I saw you." **49** Nathanael answered him, "Rabbi, you are the Son of God! You are the King of Israel!" **50** Jesus answered him, "Because I said to you, 'I saw you under the fig tree,' do you believe? You will see greater things than these." **51** And he said to him, "Truly, truly, I say to you,[11] you will see heaven opened, and the angels of God ascending and descending on the Son of Man."

> **FACT**
>
> There is one God who is Triune. See diagram on page 67.

---

10. *Cephas* and *Peter* are from the word for *rock* in Aramaic and Greek, respectively.
11. The Greek for *you* is plural; twice in this verse.

The Wedding at Cana

2 On the third day there was a wedding at Cana in Galilee, and the mother of Jesus was there. ²Jesus also was invited to the wedding with his disciples. ³When the wine ran out, the mother of Jesus said to him, "They have no wine." ⁴And Jesus said to her, "Woman, what does this have to do with me? My hour has not yet come." ⁵His mother said to the servants, "Do whatever he tells you."⁶Now there were six stone water jars there for the Jewish rites of purification, each holding twenty or thirty gallons.¹ ⁷Jesus said to the servants, "Fill the jars with water." And they filled them up to the brim. ⁸And he said to them, "Now draw some out and take it to the master of the feast." So they took it. ⁹When the master of the feast tasted the water now become wine, and did not know where it came from (though the servants who had drawn the water knew), the master of the feast called the bridegroom ¹⁰and said to him, "Everyone serves the good wine first, and when people have drunk freely, then the poor wine. But you have kept the good wine until now." ¹¹This, the first of his signs, Jesus did at Cana in Galilee, and manifested his glory. And his disciples believed in him.

¹²After this he went down to Capernaum, with his mother and his brothers² and his disciples, and they stayed there for a few days.

The first recorded miracle of Jesus in the Gospels is not turning water into wine, but is creation (John 1:1–3).

---

1. Greek *two or three measures* (*metrētas*); a *metrētēs* was about 10 gallons or 35 liters.
2. Or *brothers and sisters*. The plural Greek word *adelphoi* (translated "brothers") refers to siblings in a family. In New Testament usage, depending on the context, *adelphoi* may refer either to *brothers* or to *brothers and sisters*.

Jesus Cleanses the Temple

13 The Passover of the Jews was at hand, and Jesus went up to Jerusalem. **14** In the temple he found those who were selling oxen and sheep and pigeons, and the money-changers sitting there. **15** And making a whip of cords, he drove them all out of the temple, with the sheep and oxen. And he poured out the coins of the money-changers and overturned their tables. **16** And he told those who sold the pigeons, "Take these things away; do not make my Father's house a house of trade." **17** His disciples remembered that it was written, "Zeal for your house will consume me."

18 So the Jews said to him, "What sign do you show us for doing these things?" **19** Jesus answered them, "Destroy this temple, and in three days I will raise it up." **20** The Jews then said, "It has taken forty-six years to build this temple,³ and will you raise it up in three days?" **21** But he was speaking about the temple of his body. **22** When therefore he was raised from the dead, his disciples remembered that he had said this, and they believed the Scripture and the word that Jesus had spoken.

Jesus Knows What Is in Man

23 Now when he was in Jerusalem at the Passover Feast, many believed in his name when they saw the signs that he was doing. **24** But Jesus on his part did not entrust himself to them, because he knew all people **25** and needed no one to bear witness about man, for he himself knew what was in man.

> **cross-ref**
>
> For I delivered to you as of first importance what I also received: that Christ died for our sins in accordance with the Scriptures, that he was buried, that he was raised on the third day in accordance with the Scriptures (1 Corinthians 15:3–4).

---

3.   Or *This temple was built forty-six years ago*

You Must Be Born Again

3 Now there was a man of the Pharisees named Nicodemus, a ruler of the Jews. **2** This man came to Jesus[1] by night and said to him, "Rabbi, we know that you are a teacher come from God, for no one can do these signs that you do unless God is with him." **3** Jesus answered him, "Truly, truly, I say to you, unless one is born again[2] he cannot see the kingdom of God." **4** Nicodemus said to him, "How can a man be born when he is old? Can he enter a second time into his mother's womb and be born?" **5** Jesus answered, "Truly, truly, I say to you, unless one is born of water and the Spirit, he cannot enter the kingdom of God. **6** That which is born of the flesh is flesh, and that which is born of the Spirit is spirit.[3] **7** Do not marvel that I said to you, 'You[4] must be born again.' **8** The wind[5] blows where it wishes, and you hear its sound, but you do not know where it comes from or where it goes. So it is with everyone who is born of the Spirit." **9** Nicodemus said to him, "How can these things be?" **10** Jesus answered him, "Are you the teacher of Israel and yet you do not understand these things? **11** Truly, truly, I say to you, we speak of what we know, and bear witness to what we have seen, but you[6] do not receive our testimony. **12** If I have told you earthly things and you do not believe,

> **If the earthy things are true (e.g., the things in Genesis 1–11), the heavenly things are as well.**

---

1. Greek *him*.
2. Or *from above*; the Greek is purposely ambiguous and can mean both *again* and *from above*; also verse 7.
3. The same Greek word means both *wind* and *spirit*.
4. The Greek for *you* is plural here.
5. The same Greek word means both *wind* and *spirit*.
6. The Greek for *you* is plural here; also four times in verse 12.

how can you believe if I tell you heavenly things? [13]No one has ascended into heaven except he who descended from heaven, the Son of Man.[7] [14]And as Moses lifted up the serpent in the wilderness, so must the Son of Man be lifted up, [15]that whoever believes in him may have eternal life.[8]

For God So Loved the World

[16]"For God so loved the world,[9] that he gave his only Son, that whoever believes in him should not perish but have eternal life. [17]For God did not send his Son into the world to condemn the world, but in order that the world might be saved through him. [18]Whoever believes in him is not condemned, but whoever does not believe is condemned already, because he has not believed in the name of the only Son of God. [19]And this is the judgment: the light has come into the world, and people loved the darkness rather than the light because their works were evil. [20]For everyone who does wicked things hates the light and does not come to the light, lest his works should be exposed. [21]But whoever does what is true comes to the light, so that it may be clearly seen that his works have been carried out in God."

> The punishment from an infinite God is an infinite punishment. Jesus Christ, the Son of God who is infinite, took that punishment because of love for us.
>
> FACT

John the Baptist Exalts Christ

[22]After this Jesus and his disciples went into the Judean countryside, and he remained there with them and was baptizing. [23]John also was baptizing at Aenon

---

7. Some manuscripts add *who is in heaven.*
8. Some interpreters hold that the quotation ends at verse 15.
9. Or *For this is how God loved the world.*

near Salim, because water was plentiful there, and people were coming and being baptized [24] (for John had not yet been put in prison).

[25] Now a discussion arose between some of John's disciples and a Jew over purification. [26] And they came to John and said to him, "Rabbi, he who was with you across the Jordan, to whom you bore witness — look, he is baptizing, and all are going to him." [27] John answered, "A person cannot receive even one thing unless it is given him from heaven. [28] You yourselves bear me witness, that I said, 'I am not the Christ, but I have been sent before him.' [29] The one who has the bride is the bridegroom. The friend of the bridegroom, who stands and hears him, rejoices greatly at the bridegroom's voice. Therefore this joy of mine is now complete. [30] He must increase, but I must decrease."[10]

[31] He who comes from above is above all. He who is of the earth belongs to the earth and speaks in an earthly way. He who comes from heaven is above all. [32] He bears witness to what he has seen and heard, yet no one receives his testimony. [33] Whoever receives his testimony sets his seal to this, that God is true. [34] For he whom God has sent utters the words of God, for he gives the Spirit without measure. [35] The Father loves the Son and has given all things into his hand. [36] Whoever believes in the Son has eternal life; whoever does not obey the Son shall not see life, but the wrath of God remains on him.

cross-ref

And there is salvation in no one else, for there is no other name under heaven given among men by which we must be saved (Acts 4:12).

---

10. Some interpreters hold that the quotation continues through verse 36.

Notice the big picture. God made a perfect world and we messed it up. In the same way that the Lord sought after Adam and Eve in Genesis 3, so the Lord sought after us. God is indeed a loving, merciful, and gracious God. How much more should we love God?

By this we know that we love the children of God, when we love God and obey his commandments (1 John 5:2).

There is one God (Deuteronomy 6:4) who is Triune (three in one): God — the Father (John 1:18), God — the Son (Colossians 2:9), and God — the Holy Spirit (Acts 5:3–4).

Jesus and the Woman of Samaria

4 Now when Jesus learned that the Pharisees had heard that Jesus was making and baptizing more disciples than John ² (although Jesus himself did not baptize, but only his disciples), ³ he left Judea and departed again for Galilee. ⁴ And he had to pass through Samaria. ⁵ So he came to a town of Samaria called Sychar, near the field that Jacob had given to his son Joseph. ⁶ Jacob's well was there; so Jesus, wearied as he was from his journey, was sitting beside the well. It was about the sixth hour.[1] ⁷ A woman from Samaria came to draw water. Jesus said to her, "Give me a drink." ⁸ (For his disciples had gone away into the city to buy food.) ⁹ The Samaritan woman said to him, "How is it that you, a Jew, ask for a drink from me, a woman of Samaria?" (For Jews have no dealings with Samaritans.) ¹⁰ Jesus answered her, "If you knew the gift of God, and who it is that is saying to you, 'Give me a drink,' you would have asked him, and he would have given you living water." ¹¹ The woman said to him, "Sir, you have nothing to draw water with, and the well is deep. Where do you get that living water? ¹² Are you greater than our father Jacob? He gave us the well and drank from it himself, as did his sons and his livestock." ¹³ Jesus said to her, "Everyone who drinks of this water will be thirsty again, ¹⁴ but whoever drinks of the water that I will give him will never be thirsty again.[2] The water that I will give him will become in him a spring of water welling up to eternal life." ¹⁵ The woman said to

FACT

Omri, one of the evil kings of Israel, built Samaria on a hill (1 Kings 16:23–25). Ultimately as a result, they became a people-group of their own — separated from the Jews.

---

1. That is, about noon.
2. Greek *forever*.

him, "Sir, give me this water, so that I will not be thirsty or have to come here to draw water."

¹⁶ Jesus said to her, "Go, call your husband, and come here." ¹⁷ The woman answered him, "I have no husband." Jesus said to her, "You are right in saying, 'I have no husband'; ¹⁸for you have had five husbands, and the one you now have is not your husband. What you have said is true." ¹⁹ The woman said to him, "Sir, I perceive that you are a prophet. ²⁰ Our fathers worshiped on this mountain, but you say that in Jerusalem is the place where people ought to worship." ²¹ Jesus said to her, "Woman, believe me, the hour is coming when neither on this mountain nor in Jerusalem will you worship the Father. ²²You worship what you do not know; we worship what we know, for salvation is from the Jews. ²³But the hour is coming, and is now here, when the true worshipers will worship the Father in spirit and truth, for the Father is seeking such people to worship him. ²⁴God is spirit, and those who worship him must worship in spirit and truth." ²⁵ The woman said to him, "I know that Messiah is coming (he who is called Christ). When he comes, he will tell us all things." ²⁶ Jesus said to her, "I who speak to you am he."

²⁷ Just then his disciples came back. They marveled that he was talking with a woman, but no one said, "What do you seek?" or, "Why are you talking with her?" ²⁸ So the woman left her water jar and went away into town and said to the people, ²⁹ "Come, see a man who told me all that I ever did. Can this be the Christ?" ³⁰ They went out of the town and were coming to him.

Did you realize that this sinful Samarian woman changed her life as a result of listening to Jesus?

³¹ Meanwhile the disciples were urging him, saying, "Rabbi, eat." ³² But he said to them, "I have food to eat that you do not know about." ³³ So the disciples said to one another, "Has anyone brought him something to eat?" ³⁴ Jesus said to them, "My food is to do the will of him who sent me and to accomplish his work. ³⁵ Do you not say, 'There are yet four months, then comes the harvest'? Look, I tell you, lift up your eyes, and see that the fields are white for harvest. ³⁶ Already the one who reaps is receiving wages and gathering fruit for eternal life, so that sower and reaper may rejoice together. ³⁷ For here the saying holds true, 'One sows and another reaps.' ³⁸ I sent you to reap that for which you did not labor. Others have labored, and you have entered into their labor."

FACT

Notice the Samaritan woman's testimony — and the result!

³⁹ Many Samaritans from that town believed in him because of the woman's testimony, "He told me all that I ever did." ⁴⁰ So when the Samaritans came to him, they asked him to stay with them, and he stayed there two days. ⁴¹ And many more believed because of his word. ⁴² They said to the woman, "It is no longer because of what you said that we believe, for we have heard for ourselves, and we know that this is indeed the Savior of the world."

⁴³ After the two days he departed for Galilee. ⁴⁴ (For Jesus himself had testified that a prophet has no honor in his own hometown.) ⁴⁵ So when he came to Galilee, the Galileans welcomed him, having seen all that he had done in Jerusalem at the feast. For they too had gone to the feast.

Jesus Heals an Official's Son

46 So he came again to Cana in Galilee, where he had made the water wine. And at Capernaum there was an official whose son was ill. **47** When this man heard that Jesus had come from Judea to Galilee, he went to him and asked him to come down and heal his son, for he was at the point of death. **48** So Jesus said to him, "Unless you[3] see signs and wonders you will not believe." **49** The official said to him, "Sir, come down before my child dies." **50** Jesus said to him, "Go; your son will live." The man believed the word that Jesus spoke to him and went on his way. **51** As he was going down, his servants[4] met him and told him that his son was recovering. **52** So he asked them the hour when he began to get better, and they said to him, "Yesterday at the seventh hour[5] the fever left him." **53** The father knew that was the hour when Jesus had said to him, "Your son will live." And he himself believed, and all his household. **54** This was now the second sign that Jesus did when he had come from Judea to Galilee.

Some people criticize miracles, but if God, who created all things, is involved, why is it an issue?

---

3. The Greek for *you* is plural; twice in this verse.
4. Greek *bondservants*.
5. That is, at 1 P.M.

The Healing at the Pool on the Sabbath

5 After this there was a feast of the Jews, and Jesus went up to Jerusalem. [2] Now there is in Jerusalem by the Sheep Gate a pool, in Aramaic[1] called Bethesda,[2] which has five roofed colonnades. [3] In these lay a multitude of invalids — blind, lame, and paralyzed.[3] [5] One man was there who had been an invalid for thirty-eight years. [6] When Jesus saw him lying there and knew that he had already been there a long time, he said to him, "Do you want to be healed?" [7] The sick man answered him, "Sir, I have no one to put me into the pool when the water is stirred up, and while I am going another steps down before me." [8] Jesus said to him, "Get up, take up your bed, and walk." [9] And at once the man was healed, and he took up his bed and walked.

Now that day was the Sabbath. [10] So the Jews[4] said to the man who had been healed, "It is the Sabbath, and it is not lawful for you to take up your bed." [11] But he answered them, "The man who healed me, that man said to me, 'Take up your bed, and walk.'" [12] They asked him, "Who is the man who said to you, 'Take up your bed and walk'?" [13] Now the man who had been healed did not know who it was, for Jesus had withdrawn, as there was a crowd in the place. [14] Afterward Jesus found him in the temple and said to him, "See, you are well!

FACT

Many Pharisees were being legalistic about the rules, and did not have hearts set on God. Sadly, today many Christians do the same, but one should not judge God on the actions of people, who do still fall short.

---

1. Or *Hebrew.*

2. Some manuscripts *Bethsaida.*

3. Some manuscripts insert, wholly or in part, *waiting for the moving of the water;* [4] *for an angel of the Lord went down at certain seasons into the pool, and stirred the water: whoever stepped in first after the stirring of the water was healed of whatever disease he had.*

4. The Greek word *Ioudaioi* refers specifically here to Jewish religious leaders, and others under their influence, who opposed Jesus in that time; also verses 15, 16, 18.

Sin no more, that nothing worse may happen to you." **15** The man went away and told the Jews that it was Jesus who had healed him. **16** And this was why the Jews were persecuting Jesus, because he was doing these things on the Sabbath. **17** But Jesus answered them, "My Father is working until now, and I am working."

Jesus Is Equal with God

18 This was why the Jews were seeking all the more to kill him, because not only was he breaking the Sabbath, but he was even calling God his own Father, making himself equal with God.

The Authority of the Son

19 So Jesus said to them, "Truly, truly, I say to you, the Son can do nothing of his own accord, but only what he sees the Father doing. For whatever the Father[5] does, that the Son does likewise. **20** For the Father loves the Son and shows him all that he himself is doing. And greater works than these will he show him, so that you may marvel. **21** For as the Father raises the dead and gives them life, so also the Son gives life to whom he will. **22** The Father judges no one, but has given all judgment to the Son, **23** that all may honor the Son, just as they honor the Father. Whoever does not honor the Son does not honor the Father who sent him. **24** Truly, truly, I say to you, whoever hears my word and believes him who sent me has eternal life. He does not come into judgment, but has passed from death to life.

Jesus, who is God, has equality with God and comes with that authority (Philippians 2:5–11).

---

5. Greek *he*.

²⁵"Truly, truly, I say to you, an hour is coming, and is now here, when the dead will hear the voice of the Son of God, and those who hear will live. ²⁶For as the Father has life in himself, so he has granted the Son also to have life in himself. ²⁷And he has given him authority to execute judgment, because he is the Son of Man. ²⁸Do not marvel at this, for an hour is coming when all who are in the tombs will hear his voice ²⁹and come out, those who have done good to the resurrection of life, and those who have done evil to the resurrection of judgment.

Witnesses to Jesus

³⁰"I can do nothing on my own. As I hear, I judge, and my judgment is just, because I seek not my own will but the will of him who sent me. ³¹If I alone bear witness about myself, my testimony is not true. ³²There is another who bears witness about me, and I know that the testimony that he bears about me is true. ³³You sent to John, and he has borne witness to the truth. ³⁴Not that the testimony that I receive is from man, but I say these things so that you may be saved. ³⁵He was a burning and shining lamp, and you were willing to rejoice for a while in his light. ³⁶But the testimony that I have is greater than that of John. For the works that the Father has given me to accomplish, the very works that I am doing, bear witness about me that the Father has sent me. ³⁷And the Father who sent me has himself borne witness about me. His voice you have never heard, his form you have never seen, ³⁸and you do not have his word abiding in you, for you do not

cross-ref

And these will go away into eternal punishment, but the righteous into eternal life (Matthew 25:46).

believe the one whom he has sent. **39**You search the Scriptures because you think that in them you have eternal life; and it is they that bear witness about me, **40**yet you refuse to come to me that you may have life. **41**I do not receive glory from people. **42**But I know that you do not have the love of God within you. **43**I have come in my Father's name, and you do not receive me. If another comes in his own name, you will receive him. **44**How can you believe, when you receive glory from one another and do not seek the glory that comes from the only God? **45**Do not think that I will accuse you to the Father. There is one who accuses you: Moses, on whom you have set your hope. **46**For if you believed Moses, you would believe me; for he wrote of me. **47**But if you do not believe his writings, how will you believe my words?"

Did you realize that Moses wrote Genesis 1–11?

Jesus Feeds the Five Thousand

6 After this Jesus went away to the other side of the Sea of Galilee, which is the Sea of Tiberias. ²And a large crowd was following him, because they saw the signs that he was doing on the sick. ³Jesus went up on the mountain, and there he sat down with his disciples. ⁴Now the Passover, the feast of the Jews, was at hand. ⁵Lifting up his eyes, then, and seeing that a large crowd was coming toward him, Jesus said to Philip, "Where are we to buy bread, so that these people may eat?" ⁶He said this to test him, for he himself knew what he would do. ⁷Philip answered him, "Two hundred denarii[1] worth of bread would not be enough for each of them to get a little." ⁸One of his disciples, Andrew, Simon Peter's brother, said to him, ⁹"There is a boy here who has five barley loaves and two fish, but what are they for so many?" ¹⁰Jesus said, "Have the people sit down." Now there was much grass in the place. So the men sat down, about five thousand in number. ¹¹Jesus then took the loaves, and when he had given thanks, he distributed them to those who were seated. So also the fish, as much as they wanted. ¹²And when they had eaten their fill, he told his disciples, "Gather up the leftover fragments, that nothing may be lost." ¹³So they gathered them up and filled twelve baskets with fragments from the five barley loaves left by those who had eaten. ¹⁴When the people saw the sign that he had done, they said, "This is indeed the Prophet who is to come into the world!" ¹⁵Perceiving then that they were about to come and take him by

FACT

Notice that the 5,000 that were fed just lists the men! There were also ladies and children.

---

1. A *denarius* was a day's wage for a laborer.

force to make him king, Jesus withdrew again to the mountain by himself.

Jesus Walks on Water

16 When evening came, his disciples went down to the sea, **17** got into a boat, and started across the sea to Capernaum. It was now dark, and Jesus had not yet come to them. **18** The sea became rough because a strong wind was blowing. **19** When they had rowed about three or four miles,[2] they saw Jesus walking on the sea and coming near the boat, and they were frightened. **20** But he said to them, "It is I; do not be afraid." **21** Then they were glad to take him into the boat, and immediately the boat was at the land to which they were going.

I Am the Bread of Life

22 On the next day the crowd that remained on the other side of the sea saw that there had been only one boat there, and that Jesus had not entered the boat with his disciples, but that his disciples had gone away alone. **23** Other boats from Tiberias came near the place where they had eaten the bread after the Lord had given thanks. **24** So when the crowd saw that Jesus was not there, nor his disciples, they themselves got into the boats and went to Capernaum, seeking Jesus.

Did you know that when the Creator wants to go for a walk, water is not an obstacle!

25 When they found him on the other side of the sea, they said to him, "Rabbi, when did you come here?" **26** Jesus answered them, "Truly, truly, I say to you, you are seeking me, not because you saw signs, but because you ate your fill of the loaves. **27** Do not work for the

2.   Greek *twenty-five or thirty stadia; a stadion* was about 607 feet or 185 meters.

food that perishes, but for the food that endures to eternal life, which the Son of Man will give to you. For on him God the Father has set his seal." **28** Then they said to him, "What must we do, to be doing the works of God?" **29** Jesus answered them, "This is the work of God, that you believe in him whom he has sent." **30** So they said to him, "Then what sign do you do, that we may see and believe you? What work do you perform? **31** Our fathers ate the manna in the wilderness; as it is written, 'He gave them bread from heaven to eat.'" **32** Jesus then said to them, "Truly, truly, I say to you, it was not Moses who gave you the bread from heaven, but my Father gives you the true bread from heaven. **33** For the bread of God is he who comes down from heaven and gives life to the world." **34** They said to him, "Sir, give us this bread always."

35 Jesus said to them, "I am the bread of life; whoever comes to me shall not hunger, and whoever believes in me shall never thirst. **36** But I said to you that you have seen me and yet do not believe. **37** All that the Father gives me will come to me, and whoever comes to me I will never cast out. **38** For I have come down from heaven, not to do my own will but the will of him who sent me. **39** And this is the will of him who sent me, that I should lose nothing of all that he has given me, but raise it up on the last day. **40** For this is the will of my Father, that everyone who looks on the Son and believes in him should have eternal life, and I will raise him up on the last day."

41 So the Jews grumbled about him, because he said, "I am the bread that came down from heaven." **42** They said, "Is not this Jesus, the son of Joseph, whose

cross-ref

Notice how Jesus compares bread to Himself being the bread of Life. Recall in John 4 how Jesus compares water to Himself as living water for eternal life.

father and mother we know? How does he now say, 'I have come down from heaven'?" **43** Jesus answered them, "Do not grumble among yourselves. **44** No one can come to me unless the Father who sent me draws him. And I will raise him up on the last day. **45** It is written in the Prophets, 'And they will all be taught by God.' Everyone who has heard and learned from the Father comes to me — **46** not that anyone has seen the Father except he who is from God; he has seen the Father. **47** Truly, truly, I say to you, whoever believes has eternal life. **48** I am the bread of life. **49** Your fathers ate the manna in the wilderness, and they died. **50** This is the bread that comes down from heaven, so that one may eat of it and not die. **51** I am the living bread that came down from heaven. If anyone eats of this bread, he will live forever. And the bread that I will give for the life of the world is my flesh."

52 The Jews then disputed among themselves, saying, "How can this man give us his flesh to eat?" **53** So Jesus said to them, "Truly, truly, I say to you, unless you eat the flesh of the Son of Man and drink his blood, you have no life in you. **54** Whoever feeds on my flesh and drinks my blood has eternal life, and I will raise him up on the last day. **55** For my flesh is true food, and my blood is true drink. **56** Whoever feeds on my flesh and drinks my blood abides in me, and I in him. **57** As the living Father sent me, and I live because of the Father, so whoever feeds on me, he also will live because of me. **58** This is the bread that came down from heaven, not like the bread[3] the fathers ate, and died. Whoever feeds on this bread

> Many Jews failed to understand what Jesus was saying about the flesh and blood. Christians, in one sense, still honor this when we take communion, but it is talking about spiritual life (verse 63).

---

3. Greek lacks *the bread.*

will live forever." [59] Jesus[4] said these things in the synagogue, as he taught at Capernaum.

The Words of Eternal Life

[60] When many of his disciples heard it, they said, "This is a hard saying; who can listen to it?" [61] But Jesus, knowing in himself that his disciples were grumbling about this, said to them, "Do you take offense at this? [62] Then what if you were to see the Son of Man ascending to where he was before? [63] It is the Spirit who gives life; the flesh is no help at all. The words that I have spoken to you are spirit and life. [64] But there are some of you who do not believe." (For Jesus knew from the beginning who those were who did not believe, and who it was who would betray him.) [65] And he said, "This is why I told you that no one can come to me unless it is granted him by the Father."

[66] After this many of his disciples turned back and no longer walked with him. [67] So Jesus said to the Twelve, "Do you want to go away as well?" [68] Simon Peter answered him, "Lord, to whom shall we go? You have the words of eternal life, [69] and we have believed, and have come to know, that you are the Holy One of God." [70] Jesus answered them, "Did I not choose you, the Twelve? And yet one of you is a devil." [71] He spoke of Judas the son of Simon Iscariot, for he, one of the Twelve, was going to betray him.

FACT

Even then, Jesus knew Judas would betray Him.

---

4. Greek *He.*

Christ is eternal life. When you believe in Jesus, you too will have eternal life (John 3:16).

Then he brought them out and said, "Sirs, what must I do to be saved?" And they said, "Believe in the Lord Jesus, and you will be saved, you and your household" (Acts 16:30–31).

Jesus at the Feast of Booths

7 After this Jesus went about in Galilee. He would not go about in Judea, because the Jews[1] were seeking to kill him. **2** Now the Jews' Feast of Booths was at hand. **3** So his brothers[2] said to him, "Leave here and go to Judea, that your disciples also may see the works you are doing. **4** For no one works in secret if he seeks to be known openly. If you do these things, show yourself to the world." **5** For not even his brothers believed in him. **6** Jesus said to them, "My time has not yet come, but your time is always here. **7** The world cannot hate you, but it hates me because I testify about it that its works are evil. **8** You go up to the feast. I am not[3] going up to this feast, for my time has not yet fully come." **9** After saying this, he remained in Galilee. **10** But after his brothers had gone up to the feast, then he also went up, not publicly but in private. **11** The Jews were looking for him at the feast, and saying, "Where is he?" **12** And there was much muttering about him among the people. While some said, "He is a good man," others said, "No, he is leading the people astray." **13** Yet for fear of the Jews no one spoke openly of him.

14 About the middle of the feast Jesus went up into the temple and began teaching. **15** The Jews therefore marveled, saying, "How is it that this man has learning,[4] when he has never studied?" **16** So Jesus answered them,

cross-ref

Even Jesus silenced others when the time was not ready for Him to be known (Mark 3:11–12).

---

1. Or *Judeans*; Greek *Ioudaioi* probably refers here to Jewish religious leaders, and others under their influence, in that time.
2. Or *brothers and sisters*; also verses 5, 10.
3. Some manuscripts add *yet*.
4. Or *this man knows his letters*.

"My teaching is not mine, but his who sent me. [17]If anyone's will is to do God's[5] will, he will know whether the teaching is from God or whether I am speaking on my own authority. [18]The one who speaks on his own authority seeks his own glory; but the one who seeks the glory of him who sent him is true, and in him there is no falsehood. [19]Has not Moses given you the law? Yet none of you keeps the law. Why do you seek to kill me?" [20] The crowd answered, "You have a demon! Who is seeking to kill you?" [21]Jesus answered them, "I did one work, and you all marvel at it. [22]Moses gave you circumcision (not that it is from Moses, but from the fathers), and you circumcise a man on the Sabbath. [23]If on the Sabbath a man receives circumcision, so that the law of Moses may not be broken, are you angry with me because on the Sabbath I made a man's whole body well? [24]Do not judge by appearances, but judge with right judgment."

Can This Be the Christ?

[25]Some of the people of Jerusalem therefore said, "Is not this the man whom they seek to kill? [26] And here he is, speaking openly, and they say nothing to him! Can it be that the authorities really know that this is the Christ? [27]But we know where this man comes from, and when the Christ appears, no one will know where he comes from." [28] So Jesus proclaimed, as he taught in the temple, "You know me, and you know where I come from. But I have not come of my own accord. He who sent me is true, and him you do not

"Christ" means Messiah, whom the Jews longed for, such as in Daniel 9:25–26.

---

5. Greek *his*.

know. 29I know him, for I come from him, and he sent me." 30 So they were seeking to arrest him, but no one laid a hand on him, because his hour had not yet come. 31 Yet many of the people believed in him. They said, "When the Christ appears, will he do more signs than this man has done?"

Officers Sent to Arrest Jesus

32 The Pharisees heard the crowd muttering these things about him, and the chief priests and Pharisees sent officers to arrest him. 33 Jesus then said, "I will be with you a little longer, and then I am going to him who sent me. 34 You will seek me and you will not find me. Where I am you cannot come." 35 The Jews said to one another, "Where does this man intend to go that we will not find him? Does he intend to go to the Dispersion among the Greeks and teach the Greeks? 36 What does he mean by saying, 'You will seek me and you will not find me,' and, 'Where I am you cannot come'?"

Rivers of Living Water

37 On the last day of the feast, the great day, Jesus stood up and cried out, "If anyone thirsts, let him come to me and drink. 38 Whoever believes in me,⁶ as the Scripture has said, 'Out of his heart will flow rivers of living water.'" 39 Now this he said about the Spirit, whom those who believed in him were to receive, for as yet the Spirit had not been given, because Jesus was not yet glorified.

---

6. Or let him come to me, and let him who believes in me drink.

Division Among the People

40 When they heard these words, some of the people said, "This really is the Prophet." **41** Others said, "This is the Christ." But some said, "Is the Christ to come from Galilee? **42** Has not the Scripture said that the Christ comes from the offspring of David, and comes from Bethlehem, the village where David was?" **43** So there was a division among the people over him. **44** Some of them wanted to arrest him, but no one laid hands on him.

45 The officers then came to the chief priests and Pharisees, who said to them, "Why did you not bring him?" **46** The officers answered, "No one ever spoke like this man!" **47** The Pharisees answered them, "Have you also been deceived? **48** Have any of the authorities or the Pharisees believed in him? **49** But this crowd that does not know the law is accursed." **50** Nicodemus, who had gone to him before, and who was one of them, said to them, **51** "Does our law judge a man without first giving him a hearing and learning what he does?" **52** They replied, "Are you from Galilee too? Search and see that no prophet arises from Galilee."

Did you know that Jesus was from Bethlehem and was a direct descendent of David? Jesus grew up in Nazareth in Galilee (Luke 3, Matthew 2:1).

[The earliest manuscripts do not include 7:53–8:11.][1]

The Woman Caught in Adultery

7 **53** They went each to his own house,

8 **1** but Jesus went to the Mount of Olives. **2** Early in the morning he came again to the temple. All the people came to him, and he sat down and taught them.

3 The scribes and the Pharisees brought a woman who had been caught in adultery, and placing her in the midst **4** they said to him, "Teacher, this woman has been caught in the act of adultery. **5** Now in the Law Moses commanded us to stone such women. So what do you say?" **6** This they said to test him, that they might have some charge to bring against him. Jesus bent down and wrote with his finger on the ground. **7** And as they continued to ask him, he stood up and said to them, "Let him who is without sin among you be the first to throw a stone at her." **8** And once more he bent down and wrote on the ground. **9** But when they heard it, they went away one by one, beginning with the older ones, and Jesus was left alone with the woman standing before him. **10** Jesus stood up and said to her, "Woman, where are they? Has no one condemned you?" **11** She said, "No one, Lord." And Jesus said, "Neither do I condemn you; go, and from now on sin no more."]]

FACT

> Jesus was now the only witness. Without two witnesses, the woman was to be set free. Jesus followed the law perfectly.

I Am the Light of the World

12 Again Jesus spoke to them, saying, "I am the light of the world. Whoever follows me will not walk in

---

1. Some manuscripts do not include 7:53–8:11; others add the passage here or after 7:36 or after 21:25 or after Luke 21:38, with variations in the text.

darkness, but will have the light of life." **13** So the Pharisees said to him, "You are bearing witness about yourself; your testimony is not true." **14** Jesus answered, "Even if I do bear witness about myself, my testimony is true, for I know where I came from and where I am going, but you do not know where I come from or where I am going. **15** You judge according to the flesh; I judge no one. **16** Yet even if I do judge, my judgment is true, for it is not I alone who judge, but I and the Father[2] who sent me. **17** In your Law it is written that the testimony of two people is true. **18** I am the one who bears witness about myself, and the Father who sent me bears witness about me." **19** They said to him therefore, "Where is your Father?" Jesus answered, "You know neither me nor my Father. If you knew me, you would know my Father also." **20** These words he spoke in the treasury, as he taught in the temple; but no one arrested him, because his hour had not yet come.

21 So he said to them again, "I am going away, and you will seek me, and you will die in your sin. Where I am going, you cannot come." **22** So the Jews said, "Will he kill himself, since he says, 'Where I am going, you cannot come'?" **23** He said to them, "You are from below; I am from above. You are of this world; I am not of this world. **24** I told you that you would die in your sins, for unless you believe that I am he you will die in your sins." **25** So they said to him, "Who are you?" Jesus said to them, "Just what I have been telling you from the beginning. **26** I have much to say about you and much to judge, but he who

> **Did you know that Jesus is not of this world, as He created it — not a "space alien" as some people try to appeal to these days, but the Creator?**

---

2. Some manuscripts *he*.

sent me is true, and I declare to the world what I have heard from him." **27** They did not understand that he had been speaking to them about the Father. **28** So Jesus said to them, "When you have lifted up the Son of Man, then you will know that I am he, and that I do nothing on my own authority, but speak just as the Father taught me. **29** And he who sent me is with me. He has not left me alone, for I always do the things that are pleasing to him." **30** As he was saying these things, many believed in him.

FACT

True freedom comes with Christ — not money, not a nice job, not a nice house or car, but with Christ.

The Truth Will Set You Free

31 So Jesus said to the Jews who had believed him, "If you abide in my word, you are truly my disciples, **32** and you will know the truth, and the truth will set you free." **33** They answered him, "We are offspring of Abraham and have never been enslaved to anyone. How is it that you say, 'You will become free'?"

34 Jesus answered them, "Truly, truly, I say to you, everyone who practices sin is a slave[3] to sin. **35** The slave does not remain in the house forever; the son remains forever. **36** So if the Son sets you free, you will be free indeed. **37** I know that you are offspring of Abraham; yet you seek to kill me because my word finds no place in you. **38** I speak of what I have seen with my Father, and you do what you have heard from your father."

You Are of Your Father the Devil

39 They answered him, "Abraham is our father." Jesus said to them, "If you were Abraham's children,

---

3. Greek *bondservant*; also verse 35.

you would be doing the works Abraham did, **40**but now you seek to kill me, a man who has told you the truth that I heard from God. This is not what Abraham did. **41**You are doing the works your father did." They said to him, "We were not born of sexual immorality. We have one Father — even God." **42**Jesus said to them, "If God were your Father, you would love me, for I came from God and I am here. I came not of my own accord, but he sent me. **43**Why do you not understand what I say? It is because you cannot bear to hear my word. **44**You are of your father the devil, and your will is to do your father's desires. He was a murderer from the beginning, and does not stand in the truth, because there is no truth in him. When he lies, he speaks out of his own character, for he is a liar and the father of lies. **45**But because I tell the truth, you do not believe me. **46**Which one of you convicts me of sin? If I tell the truth, why do you not believe me? **47**Whoever is of God hears the words of God. The reason why you do not hear them is that you are not of God."

Before Abraham Was, I Am

48 The Jews answered him, "Are we not right in saying that you are a Samaritan and have a demon?" **49**Jesus answered, "I do not have a demon, but I honor my Father, and you dishonor me. **50**Yet I do not seek my own glory; there is One who seeks it, and he is the judge. **51**Truly, truly, I say to you, if anyone keeps my word, he will never see death." **52** The Jews said to him, "Now we know that you have a demon! Abraham died, as did the prophets, yet you say,

What does Jesus reveal about life and death in these verses?

'If anyone keeps my word, he will never taste death.' **53** Are you greater than our father Abraham, who died? And the prophets died! Who do you make yourself out to be?" **54** Jesus answered, "If I glorify myself, my glory is nothing. It is my Father who glorifies me, of whom you say, 'He is our God.'⁴ **55** But you have not known him. I know him. If I were to say that I do not know him, I would be a liar like you, but I do know him and I keep his word. **56** Your father Abraham rejoiced that he would see my day. He saw it and was glad." **57** So the Jews said to him, "You are not yet fifty years old, and have you seen Abraham?"⁵ **58** Jesus said to them, "Truly, truly, I say to you, before Abraham was, I am."

59 So they picked up stones to throw at him, but Jesus hid himself and went out of the temple.

FACT

Jehovah, one of the Hebrew names for God in the Old Testament, is derived from "I am." When Jesus says, "I am," He is claiming to be God.

---

4. Some manuscripts *your God.*
5. Some manuscripts *has Abraham seen you?*

Notice how Jesus followed the letter of the law perfectly when challenged? Jesus knew the accusers of the adultrous woman were sinning with her in her adultery. Jesus knew that the law required taking the life of both who were involved in adultery (the man and the woman), so he asked for the one who was without sin to cast the first stone! Then each left, knowing they too should be killed. So this only left Jesus, and yet two witnesses were required. If Jesus fulfilled the law to the letter, how much more did He fulfill the rest.

Do not think that I have come to abolish the Law or the Prophets; I have not come to abolish them but to fulfill them (Matthew 5:17).

Jesus Heals a Man Born Blind

9 As he passed by, he saw a man blind from birth. **2** And his disciples asked him, "Rabbi, who sinned, this man or his parents, that he was born blind?" **3** Jesus answered, "It was not that this man sinned, or his parents, but that the works of God might be displayed in him. **4** We must work the works of him who sent me while it is day; night is coming, when no one can work. **5** As long as I am in the world, I am the light of the world." **6** Having said these things, he spit on the ground and made mud with the saliva. Then he anointed the man's eyes with the mud **7** and said to him, "Go, wash in the pool of Siloam" (which means Sent). So he went and washed and came back seeing. **8** The neighbors and those who had seen him before as a beggar were saying, "Is this not the man who used to sit and beg?" **9** Some said, "It is he." Others said, "No, but he is like him." He kept saying, "I am the man." **10** So they said to him, "Then how were your eyes opened?" **11** He answered, "The man called Jesus made mud and anointed my eyes and said to me, 'Go to Siloam and wash.' So I went and washed and received my sight." **12** They said to him, "Where is he?" He said, "I do not know."

13 They brought to the Pharisees the man who had formerly been blind. **14** Now it was a Sabbath day when Jesus made the mud and opened his eyes. **15** So the Pharisees again asked him how he had received his sight. And he said to them, "He put mud on my eyes, and I washed, and I see." **16** Some of the Pharisees said, "This man is not from God, for he does not keep the

> Jesus answered perfectly that it was not his sin or that of his parents that caused him to be born blind. It was Adam and Eve's sin! And the works of God can undo the results of sin.

Sabbath." But others said, "How can a man who is a sinner do such signs?" And there was a division among them. **17** So they said again to the blind man, "What do you say about him, since he has opened your eyes?" He said, "He is a prophet."

18 The Jews[1] did not believe that he had been blind and had received his sight, until they called the parents of the man who had received his sight **19** and asked them, "Is this your son, who you say was born blind? How then does he now see?" **20** His parents answered, "We know that this is our son and that he was born blind. **21** But how he now sees we do not know, nor do we know who opened his eyes. Ask him; he is of age. He will speak for himself." **22** (His parents said these things because they feared the Jews, for the Jews had already agreed that if anyone should confess Jesus[2] to be Christ, he was to be put out of the synagogue.) **23** Therefore his parents said, "He is of age; ask him."

24 So for the second time they called the man who had been blind and said to him, "Give glory to God. We know that this man is a sinner." **25** He answered, "Whether he is a sinner I do not know. One thing I do know, that though I was blind, now I see." **26** They said to him, "What did he do to you? How did he open your eyes?" **27** He answered them, "I have told you already, and you would not listen. Why do you want to hear it again? Do you also want to become his disciples?" **28** And they reviled him, saying, "You are his disciple, but we are disciples of Moses.

> **FACT**
> A prophet is someone chosen by God to tell of things to come.

---

1. Greek *Ioudaioi* probably refers here to Jewish religious leaders, and others under their influence, in that time; also verse 22.
2. Greek *him*.

29 We know that God has spoken to Moses, but as for this man, we do not know where he comes from." **30** The man answered, "Why, this is an amazing thing! You do not know where he comes from, and yet he opened my eyes. **31** We know that God does not listen to sinners, but if anyone is a worshiper of God and does his will, God listens to him. **32** Never since the world began has it been heard that anyone opened the eyes of a man born blind. **33** If this man were not from God, he could do nothing." **34** They answered him, "You were born in utter sin, and would you teach us?" And they cast him out.

> **FACT**
>
> The man worshiped Jesus and Jesus did not rebuke him. Jesus, being God, accepts worship.

35 Jesus heard that they had cast him out, and having found him he said, "Do you believe in the Son of Man?"³ **36** He answered, "And who is he, sir, that I may believe in him?" **37** Jesus said to him, "You have seen him, and it is he who is speaking to you." **38** He said, "Lord, I believe," and he worshiped him. **39** Jesus said, "For judgment I came into this world, that those who do not see may see, and those who see may become blind." **40** Some of the Pharisees near him heard these things, and said to him, "Are we also blind?" **41** Jesus said to them, "If you were blind, you would have no guilt;⁴ but now that you say, 'We see,' your guilt remains.

---

3. Some manuscripts *the Son of God.*
4. Greek *you would not have sin.*

John, the author of the book, was one of Jesus' Apostles and was an eyewitness to these events. How was John's reaction to Jesus' teaching different from many Jews?

_____

_____

_____

_____

_____

_____

_____

_____

_____

_____

_____

John was often described as the disciple who Jesus loved (see John 21:20).

_____

_____

_____

_____

_____

_____

I Am the Good Shepherd

10 "Truly, truly, I say to you, he who does not enter the sheepfold by the door but climbs in by another way, that man is a thief and a robber. ²But he who enters by the door is the shepherd of the sheep. ³To him the gatekeeper opens. The sheep hear his voice, and he calls his own sheep by name and leads them out. ⁴When he has brought out all his own, he goes before them, and the sheep follow him, for they know his voice. ⁵A stranger they will not follow, but they will flee from him, for they do not know the voice of strangers." ⁶This figure of speech Jesus used with them, but they did not understand what he was saying to them. ⁷So Jesus again said to them, "Truly, truly, I say to you, I am the door of the sheep. ⁸All who came before me are thieves and robbers, but the sheep did not listen to them. ⁹I am the door. If anyone enters by me, he will be saved and will go in and out and find pasture. ¹⁰The thief comes only to steal and kill and destroy. I came that they may have life and have it abundantly. ¹¹I am the good shepherd. The good shepherd lays down his life for the sheep. ¹²He who is a hired hand and not a shepherd, who does not own the sheep, sees the wolf coming and leaves the sheep and flees, and the wolf snatches them and scatters them. ¹³He flees because he is a hired hand and cares nothing for the sheep. ¹⁴I am the good shepherd. I know my own and my own know me, ¹⁵just as the Father knows me and I know the Father; and I lay down my life for the sheep. ¹⁶And I have other sheep that are not of this fold. I must bring them also, and they will listen to my

FACT

Jesus, the good shepherd, did lay down His life for His sheep. He died for us.

voice. So there will be one flock, one shepherd. **17** For this reason the Father loves me, because I lay down my life that I may take it up again. **18** No one takes it from me, but I lay it down of my own accord. I have authority to lay it down, and I have authority to take it up again. This charge I have received from my Father."

19 There was again a division among the Jews because of these words. **20** Many of them said, "He has a demon, and is insane; why listen to him?" **21** Others said, "These are not the words of one who is oppressed by a demon. Can a demon open the eyes of the blind?"

I and the Father Are One

22 At that time the Feast of Dedication took place at Jerusalem. It was winter, **23** and Jesus was walking in the temple, in the colonnade of Solomon. **24** So the Jews gathered around him and said to him, "How long will you keep us in suspense? If you are the Christ, tell us plainly." **25** Jesus answered them, "I told you, and you do not believe. The works that I do in my Father's name bear witness about me, **26** but you do not believe because you are not among my sheep. **27** My sheep hear my voice, and I know them, and they follow me. **28** I give them eternal life, and they will never perish, and no one will snatch them out of my hand. **29** My Father, who has given them to me,[1] is greater than all, and no one is able to snatch them out of the Father's hand. **30** I and the Father are one."

31 The Jews picked up stones again to stone him. **32** Jesus answered them, "I have shown you many good

Have you considered giving your life to Christ?

---

1. Some manuscripts *What my Father has given to me.*

works from the Father; for which of them are you going to stone me?" 33 The Jews answered him, "It is not for a good work that we are going to stone you but for blasphemy, because you, being a man, make yourself God." 34 Jesus answered them, "Is it not written in your Law, 'I said, you are gods'? 35 If he called them gods to whom the word of God came — and Scripture cannot be broken — 36 do you say of him whom the Father consecrated and sent into the world, 'You are blaspheming,' because I said, 'I am the Son of God'? 37 If I am not doing the works of my Father, then do not believe me; 38 but if I do them, even though you do not believe me, believe the works, that you may know and understand that the Father is in me and I am in the Father." 39 Again they sought to arrest him, but he escaped from their hands.

40 He went away again across the Jordan to the place where John had been baptizing at first, and there he remained. 41 And many came to him. And they said, "John did no sign, but everything that John said about this man was true." 42 And many believed in him there.

FACT

We sometimes think our lives are difficult — but consider how Jesus was being threatened over and over again.

Jesus, being God in the flesh, had every right to say that He and the Father are one. He also had the right to claim that He was the Son of God. The real question is, who were the Jews to claim otherwise?

> But I say to you who hear, Love your enemies, do good to those who hate you, bless those who curse you, pray for those who abuse you (Luke 6:27–28).

The Death of Lazarus

11 Now a certain man was ill, Lazarus of Bethany, the village of Mary and her sister Martha. ²It was Mary who anointed the Lord with ointment and wiped his feet with her hair, whose brother Lazarus was ill. ³So the sisters sent to him, saying, "Lord, he whom you love is ill." ⁴But when Jesus heard it he said, "This illness does not lead to death. It is for the glory of God, so that the Son of God may be glorified through it." ⁵Now Jesus loved Martha and her sister and Lazarus. ⁶So, when he heard that Lazarus[1] was ill, he stayed two days longer in the place where he was. ⁷Then after this he said to the disciples, "Let us go to Judea again." ⁸The disciples said to him, "Rabbi, the Jews were just now seeking to stone you, and are you going there again?" ⁹Jesus answered, "Are there not twelve hours in the day? If anyone walks in the day, he does not stumble, because he sees the light of this world. ¹⁰But if anyone walks in the night, he stumbles, because the light is not in him." ¹¹After saying these things, he said to them, "Our friend Lazarus has fallen asleep, but I go to awaken him." ¹²The disciples said to him, "Lord, if he has fallen asleep, he will recover." ¹³Now Jesus had spoken of his death, but they thought that he meant taking rest in sleep. ¹⁴Then Jesus told them plainly, "Lazarus has died, ¹⁵and for your sake I am glad that I was not there, so that you may believe. But let us go to him." ¹⁶So Thomas, called the Twin,[2] said to his fellow disciples, "Let us also go, that we may die with him."

FACT

When Jesus arrived, Lazarus had been dead for four days!

---

1. Greek *he*; also verse 17.
2. Greek *Didymus*.

I Am the Resurrection and the Life

17 Now when Jesus came, he found that Lazarus had already been in the tomb four days. **18** Bethany was near Jerusalem, about two miles[3] off, **19** and many of the Jews had come to Martha and Mary to console them concerning their brother. **20** So when Martha heard that Jesus was coming, she went and met him, but Mary remained seated in the house. **21** Martha said to Jesus, "Lord, if you had been here, my brother would not have died. **22** But even now I know that whatever you ask from God, God will give you." **23** Jesus said to her, "Your brother will rise again." **24** Martha said to him, "I know that he will rise again in the resurrection on the last day." **25** Jesus said to her, "I am the resurrection and the life.[4] Whoever believes in me, though he die, yet shall he live, **26** and everyone who lives and believes in me shall never die. Do you believe this?" **27** She said to him, "Yes, Lord; I believe that you are the Christ, the Son of God, who is coming into the world."

Jesus Weeps

28 When she had said this, she went and called her sister Mary, saying in private, "The Teacher is here and is calling for you." **29** And when she heard it, she rose quickly and went to him. **30** Now Jesus had not yet come into the village, but was still in the place where Martha had met him. **31** When the Jews who were with her in the house, consoling her, saw Mary rise quickly and go out, they followed her, supposing that she was going to the tomb to weep there. **32** Now when Mary came to where

Mary and Martha were surely devastated at the death of their brother and truly believed Jesus could have healed him; however, did they realize that Jesus also had power over death?

---

3. Greek *fifteen stadia*; a stadion was about 607 feet or 185 meters.
4. Some manuscripts omit *and the life*.

Jesus was and saw him, she fell at his feet, saying to him, "Lord, if you had been here, my brother would not have died." **33** When Jesus saw her weeping, and the Jews who had come with her also weeping, he was deeply moved[5] in his spirit and greatly troubled. **34** And he said, "Where have you laid him?" They said to him, "Lord, come and see." **35** Jesus wept. **36** So the Jews said, "See how he loved him!" **37** But some of them said, "Could not he who opened the eyes of the blind man also have kept this man from dying?"

> **FACT**
>
> **Jesus has power over death and we as Christians will be alive with God forever.**

Jesus Raises Lazarus

38 Then Jesus, deeply moved again, came to the tomb. It was a cave, and a stone lay against it. **39** Jesus said, "Take away the stone." Martha, the sister of the dead man, said to him, "Lord, by this time there will be an odor, for he has been dead four days." **40** Jesus said to her, "Did I not tell you that if you believed you would see the glory of God?" **41** So they took away the stone. And Jesus lifted up his eyes and said, "Father, I thank you that you have heard me. **42** I knew that you always hear me, but I said this on account of the people standing around, that they may believe that you sent me." **43** When he had said these things, he cried out with a loud voice, "Lazarus, come out." **44** The man who had died came out, his hands and feet bound with linen strips, and his face wrapped with a cloth. Jesus said to them, "Unbind him, and let him go."

The Plot to Kill Jesus

45 Many of the Jews therefore, who had come with Mary and had seen what he did, believed in him, **46** but

5. Or *was indignant*; also verse 38.

some of them went to the Pharisees and told them what Jesus had done. **47** So the chief priests and the Pharisees gathered the council and said, "What are we to do? For this man performs many signs. **48** If we let him go on like this, everyone will believe in him, and the Romans will come and take away both our place and our nation." **49** But one of them, Caiaphas, who was high priest that year, said to them, "You know nothing at all. **50** Nor do you understand that it is better for you that one man should die for the people, not that the whole nation should perish." **51** He did not say this of his own accord, but being high priest that year he prophesied that Jesus would die for the nation, **52** and not for the nation only, but also to gather into one the children of God who are scattered abroad. **53** So from that day on they made plans to put him to death.

54 Jesus therefore no longer walked openly among the Jews, but went from there to the region near the wilderness, to a town called Ephraim, and there he stayed with the disciples.

55 Now the Passover of the Jews was at hand, and many went up from the country to Jerusalem before the Passover to purify themselves. **56** They were looking for[6] Jesus and saying to one another as they stood in the temple, "What do you think? That he will not come to the feast at all?" **57** Now the chief priests and the Pharisees had given orders that if anyone knew where he was, he should let them know, so that they might arrest him.

> The Passover was a yearly festival of the Jews to celebrate the Lord bringing them out of Egypt during the Exodus. They were to sacrifice an unblemished lamb for the feast. Jesus was sacrificed on Passover as our "unblemished lamb."

---

6. Greek *were seeking for.*

Mary Anoints Jesus at Bethany

12 Six days before the Passover, Jesus therefore came to Bethany, where Lazarus was, whom Jesus had raised from the dead. **2** So they gave a dinner for him there. Martha served, and Lazarus was one of those reclining with him at table. **3** Mary therefore took a pound[1] of expensive ointment made from pure nard, and anointed the feet of Jesus and wiped his feet with her hair. The house was filled with the fragrance of the perfume. **4** But Judas Iscariot, one of his disciples (he who was about to betray him), said, **5** "Why was this ointment not sold for three hundred denarii[2] and given to the poor?" **6** He said this, not because he cared about the poor, but because he was a thief, and having charge of the moneybag he used to help himself to what was put into it. **7** Jesus said, "Leave her alone, so that she may keep it[3] for the day of my burial. **8** For the poor you always have with you, but you do not always have me."

FACT

Judas's greed led to his downfall later on. We, too, need to watch out that we don't have greed for money.

The Plot to Kill Lazarus

9 When the large crowd of the Jews learned that Jesus[4] was there, they came, not only on account of him but also to see Lazarus, whom he had raised from the dead. **10** So the chief priests made plans to put Lazarus to death as well, **11** because on account of him many of the Jews were going away and believing in Jesus.

1. Greek *litra*; a *litra* (or Roman pound) was equal to about 11 1/2 ounces or 327 grams.
2. A *denarius* was a day's wage for a laborer.
3. Or *Leave her alone; she intended to keep it.*
4. Greek *he.*

The Triumphal Entry

12 The next day the large crowd that had come to the feast heard that Jesus was coming to Jerusalem. **13** So they took branches of palm trees and went out to meet him, crying out, "Hosanna! Blessed is he who comes in the name of the Lord, even the King of Israel!" **14** And Jesus found a young donkey and sat on it, just as it is written,

> **15** "Fear not, daughter of Zion;
> behold, your king is coming,
> sitting on a donkey's colt!"

16 His disciples did not understand these things at first, but when Jesus was glorified, then they remembered that these things had been written about him and had been done to him. **17** The crowd that had been with him when he called Lazarus out of the tomb and raised him from the dead continued to bear witness. **18** The reason why the crowd went to meet him was that they heard he had done this sign. **19** So the Pharisees said to one another, "You see that you are gaining nothing. Look, the world has gone after him."

Did you realize that Jesus knew that the time was finally at hand?

Some Greeks Seek Jesus

20 Now among those who went up to worship at the feast were some Greeks. **21** So these came to Philip, who was from Bethsaida in Galilee, and asked him, "Sir, we wish to see Jesus." **22** Philip went and told Andrew; Andrew and Philip went and told Jesus. **23** And Jesus answered them, "The hour has come for the Son of

Man to be glorified. 24Truly, truly, I say to you, unless a grain of wheat falls into the earth and dies, it remains alone; but if it dies, it bears much fruit. 25Whoever loves his life loses it, and whoever hates his life in this world will keep it for eternal life. 26If anyone serves me, he must follow me; and where I am, there will my servant be also. If anyone serves me, the Father will honor him.

The Son of Man Must Be Lifted Up

27"Now is my soul troubled. And what shall I say? 'Father, save me from this hour'? But for this purpose I have come to this hour. 28Father, glorify your name." Then a voice came from heaven: "I have glorified it, and I will glorify it again." 29 The crowd that stood there and heard it said that it had thundered. Others said, "An angel has spoken to him." 30Jesus answered, "This voice has come for your sake, not mine. 31Now is the judgment of this world; now will the ruler of this world be cast out. 32And I, when I am lifted up from the earth, will draw all people to myself." 33 He said this to show by what kind of death he was going to die. 34 So the crowd answered him, "We have heard from the Law that the Christ remains forever. How can you say that the Son of Man must be lifted up? Who is this Son of Man?" 35 So Jesus said to them, "The light is among you for a little while longer. Walk while you have the light, lest darkness overtake you. The one who walks in the darkness does not know where he is going. 36While you have the light, believe in the light, that you may become sons of light."

cross-ref

For the Son of Man goes as it is written of him, but woe to that man by whom the Son of Man is betrayed! It would have been better for that man if he had not been born (Mark 14:21).

The Unbelief of the People

When Jesus had said these things, he departed and hid himself from them. **37** Though he had done so many signs before them, they still did not believe in him, **38** so that the word spoken by the prophet Isaiah might be fulfilled:

> "Lord, who has believed what he heard from us,
> and to whom has the arm of the Lord been revealed?"

39 Therefore they could not believe. For again Isaiah said,

> **40** "He has blinded their eyes
> and hardened their heart,
> lest they see with their eyes,
> and understand with their heart, and turn,
> and I would heal them."

41 Isaiah said these things because he saw his glory and spoke of him. **42** Nevertheless, many even of the authorities believed in him, but for fear of the Pharisees they did not confess it, so that they would not be put out of the synagogue; **43** for they loved the glory that comes from man more than the glory that comes from God.

> Did you notice how the New Testament is consistent and builds on the Old Testament?

Jesus Came to Save the World

44 And Jesus cried out and said, "Whoever believes in me, believes not in me but in him who sent me. **45** And whoever sees me sees him who sent me. **46** I have come into the world as light, so that whoever believes in me may not remain in darkness. **47**If anyone hears my words and does not keep them, I do not judge him; for I did not come to judge the world but to save the world. **48**The one who rejects me and does not receive my words has a judge; the word that I have spoken will judge him on the last day. **49**For I have not spoken on my own authority, but the Father who sent me has himself given me a commandment — what to say and what to speak. **50**And I know that his commandment is eternal life. What I say, therefore, I say as the Father has told me."

FACT

The Word of God will judge our sin. When in Christ, your sin is covered.

Have you noticed how Jesus knows what will happen and permits it to happen so that the Scriptures come true? Aren't you glad that Christ went through this, so that we can be saved?

Was it not necessary that the Christ should suffer these things and enter into his glory? (Luke 24:26).

Jesus Washes the Disciples' Feet

13 Now before the Feast of the Passover, when Jesus knew that his hour had come to depart out of this world to the Father, having loved his own who were in the world, he loved them to the end. ² During supper, when the devil had already put it into the heart of Judas Iscariot, Simon's son, to betray him, ³ Jesus, knowing that the Father had given all things into his hands, and that he had come from God and was going back to God, ⁴ rose from supper. He laid aside his outer garments, and taking a towel, tied it around his waist. ⁵ Then he poured water into a basin and began to wash the disciples' feet and to wipe them with the towel that was wrapped around him. ⁶ He came to Simon Peter, who said to him, "Lord, do you wash my feet?" ⁷ Jesus answered him, "What I am doing you do not understand now, but afterward you will understand." ⁸ Peter said to him, "You shall never wash my feet." Jesus answered him, "If I do not wash you, you have no share with me." ⁹ Simon Peter said to him, "Lord, not my feet only but also my hands and my head!" ¹⁰ Jesus said to him, "The one who has bathed does not need to wash, except for his feet,¹ but is completely clean. And you² are clean, but not every one of you." ¹¹ For he knew who was to betray him; that was why he said, "Not all of you are clean." ¹² When he had washed their feet and put on his outer garments and resumed his place, he said to them, "Do you understand what I have done to you? ¹³ You call me Teacher and Lord, and you are right, for so I am. ¹⁴ If

FACT

In verse 8, Jesus uses a literal event to discuss a greater metaphor. He is washing us clean from sin.

---

1   Some manuscripts omit *except for his feet.*
2   The Greek words for *you* in this verse are plural.

I then, your Lord and Teacher, have washed your feet, you also ought to wash one another's feet. **15**For I have given you an example, that you also should do just as I have done to you. **16**Truly, truly, I say to you, a servant[3] is not greater than his master, nor is a messenger greater than the one who sent him. **17**If you know these things, blessed are you if you do them. **18**I am not speaking of all of you; I know whom I have chosen. But the Scripture will be fulfilled,[4] 'He who ate my bread has lifted his heel against me.' **19**I am telling you this now, before it takes place, that when it does take place you may believe that I am he. **20**Truly, truly, I say to you, whoever receives the one I send receives me, and whoever receives me receives the one who sent me."

One of You Will Betray Me

21 After saying these things, Jesus was troubled in his spirit, and testified, "Truly, truly, I say to you, one of you will betray me." **22** The disciples looked at one another, uncertain of whom he spoke. **23** One of his disciples, whom Jesus loved, was reclining at table at Jesus' side,[5] **24** so Simon Peter motioned to him to ask Jesus[6] of whom he was speaking. **25** So that disciple, leaning back against Jesus, said to him, "Lord, who is it?" **26** Jesus answered, "It is he to whom I will give this morsel of bread when I have dipped it." So when he had dipped the morsel, he gave it to Judas, the son of Simon Iscariot. **27** Then after he had taken the

For the Son of Man goes as it has been determined, but woe to that man by whom he is betrayed! (Luke 22:22).

cross-ref

---

3   Greek *bondservant.*
4   Greek *But in order that the Scripture may be fulfilled.*
5   Greek *in the bosom of Jesus.*
6   Greek lacks *Jesus.*

morsel, Satan entered into him. Jesus said to him, "What you are going to do, do quickly." **28** Now no one at the table knew why he said this to him. **29** Some thought that, because Judas had the moneybag, Jesus was telling him, "Buy what we need for the feast," or that he should give something to the poor. **30** So, after receiving the morsel of bread, he immediately went out. And it was night.

A New Commandment

31 When he had gone out, Jesus said, "Now is the Son of Man glorified, and God is glorified in him. **32** If God is glorified in him, God will also glorify him in himself, and glorify him at once. **33** Little children, yet a little while I am with you. You will seek me, and just as I said to the Jews, so now I also say to you, 'Where I am going you cannot come.' **34** A new commandment I give to you, that you love one another: just as I have loved you, you also are to love one another. **35** By this all people will know that you are my disciples, if you have love for one another."

Jesus Foretells Peter's Denial

36 Simon Peter said to him, "Lord, where are you going?" Jesus answered him, "Where I am going you cannot follow me now, but you will follow afterward." **37** Peter said to him, "Lord, why can I not follow you now? I will lay down my life for you." **38** Jesus answered, "Will you lay down your life for me? Truly, truly, I say to you, the rooster will not crow till you have denied me three times.

FACT

Building on Leviticus 19:18, Christ's new commandment was to love as He had.

Satan entered the serpent in Genesis 3; we see his actions with the evil king of Tyre in Ezekiel 28 and even entering Peter in Mark 8:33. Now we see Judas, with Satan entering him, attacking and betraying Christ. How would you feel if one of your close associates betrayed you with lies?

_____

_____

_____

_____

_____

_____

_____

_____

_____

_____

_____

Then one of the twelve, whose name was Judas Iscariot, went to the chief priests and said, "What will you give me if I deliver him over to you?" And they paid him thirty pieces of silver (Matthew 26:14–15).

_____

_____

_____

_____

_____

I Am the Way, and the Truth, and the Life

14 "Let not your hearts be troubled. Believe in God;[1] believe also in me. **2** In my Father's house are many rooms. If it were not so, would I have told you that I go to prepare a place for you?[2] **3** And if I go and prepare a place for you, I will come again and will take you to myself, that where I am you may be also. **4** And you know the way to where I am going."[3] **5** Thomas said to him, "Lord, we do not know where you are going. How can we know the way?" **6** Jesus said to him, "I am the way, and the truth, and the life. No one comes to the Father except through me. **7** If you had known me, you would have known my Father also.[4] From now on you do know him and have seen him." **8** Philip said to him, "Lord, show us the Father, and it is enough for us." **9** Jesus said to him, "Have I been with you so long, and you still do not know me, Philip? Whoever has seen me has seen the Father. How can you say, 'Show us the Father'? **10** Do you not believe that I am in the Father and the Father is in me? The words that I say to you I do not speak on my own authority, but the Father who dwells in me does his works. **11** Believe me that I am in the Father and the Father is in me, or else believe on account of the works themselves.

12 "Truly, truly, I say to you, whoever believes in me will also do the works that I do; and greater works than

cross-ref

Because, if you confess with your mouth that Jesus is Lord and believe in your heart that God raised him from the dead, you will be saved (Romans 10:9).

---

1. Or *You believe in God.*
2. Or *In my Father's house are many rooms; if it were not so, I would have told you; for I go to prepare a place for you.*
3. Some manuscripts *Where I am going you know, and the way you know.*
4. Or *If you know me, you will know my Father also,* or *If you have known me, you will know my Father also.*

these will he do, because I am going to the Father. **13** Whatever you ask in my name, this I will do, that the Father may be glorified in the Son. **14** If you ask me[5] anything in my name, I will do it.

Jesus Promises the Holy Spirit

15 "If you love me, you will keep my commandments. **16** And I will ask the Father, and he will give you another Helper,[6] to be with you forever, **17** even the Spirit of truth, whom the world cannot receive, because it neither sees him nor knows him. You know him, for he dwells with you and will be[7] in you.

18 "I will not leave you as orphans; I will come to you. **19** Yet a little while and the world will see me no more, but you will see me. Because I live, you also will live. **20** In that day you will know that I am in my Father, and you in me, and I in you. **21** Whoever has my commandments and keeps them, he it is who loves me. And he who loves me will be loved by my Father, and I will love him and manifest myself to him." **22** Judas (not Iscariot) said to him, "Lord, how is it that you will manifest yourself to us, and not to the world?" **23** Jesus answered him, "If anyone loves me, he will keep my word, and my Father will love him, and we will come to him and make our home with him. **24** Whoever does not love me does not keep my words. And the word that you hear is not mine but the Father's who sent me.

Did you know that when we receive Christ, we receive the gift of the Holy Spirit living in us?

---

5. Some manuscripts omit *me*.

6. Or *Advocate*, or *Counselor*; also 14:26; 15:26; 16:7.

7. Some manuscripts *and is*.

25 "These things I have spoken to you while I am still with you. 26 But the Helper, the Holy Spirit, whom the Father will send in my name, he will teach you all things and bring to your remembrance all that I have said to you. 27 Peace I leave with you; my peace I give to you. Not as the world gives do I give to you. Let not your hearts be troubled, neither let them be afraid. 28 You heard me say to you, 'I am going away, and I will come to you.' If you loved me, you would have rejoiced, because I am going to the Father, for the Father is greater than I. 29 And now I have told you before it takes place, so that when it does take place you may believe. 30 I will no longer talk much with you, for the ruler of this world is coming. He has no claim on me, 31 but I do as the Father has commanded me, so that the world may know that I love the Father. Rise, let us go from here.

cross-ref

When Jesus says "the Father is greater than I," he is referring to this comparison while being in an humbled, unglorified state (i.e., His human state — Philippians 2:8). Upon the Resurrection, Christ is reglorified (Philippians 2:9).

Christ is above all, and yet He came down and "emptied Himself" and became obedient to death on a cross. Yet He conquered death, showing that we, too, can conquer death through Christ. We will all die once, but death will have "no sting" for those in Christ.

And just as it is appointed for man to die once, and after that comes judgment (Hebrews 9:27).
O death, where is your victory? O death, where is your sting?
(1 Corinthians 15:55).

I Am the True Vine

15 "I am the true vine, and my Father is the vinedresser. **2** Every branch in me that does not bear fruit he takes away, and every branch that does bear fruit he prunes, that it may bear more fruit. **3** Already you are clean because of the word that I have spoken to you. **4** Abide in me, and I in you. As the branch cannot bear fruit by itself, unless it abides in the vine, neither can you, unless you abide in me. **5** I am the vine; you are the branches. Whoever abides in me and I in him, he it is that bears much fruit, for apart from me you can do nothing. **6** If anyone does not abide in me he is thrown away like a branch and withers; and the branches are gathered, thrown into the fire, and burned. **7** If you abide in me, and my words abide in you, ask whatever you wish, and it will be done for you. **8** By this my Father is glorified, that you bear much fruit and so prove to be my disciples. **9** As the Father has loved me, so have I loved you. Abide in my love. **10** If you keep my commandments, you will abide in my love, just as I have kept my Father's commandments and abide in his love. **11** These things I have spoken to you, that my joy may be in you, and that your joy may be full.

12 "This is my commandment, that you love one another as I have loved you. **13** Greater love has no one than this, that someone lay down his life for his friends. **14** You are my friends if you do what I command you. **15** No longer do I call you servants,[1] for the servant[2] does not know what his master is doing; but I have called you friends, for all that I have heard from my Father I have

> **FACT**
>
> Jesus often spoke in metaphors and parables, but that doesn't mean the whole Bible is a metaphor. It is written in various literary styles and should be read as such — literal history is literal history; metaphors are metaphors, etc.

---

1. Greek *bondservants*.
2. Greek *bondservant*; also verse 20.

made known to you. **16** You did not choose me, but I chose you and appointed you that you should go and bear fruit and that your fruit should abide, so that whatever you ask the Father in my name, he may give it to you. **17** These things I command you, so that you will love one another.

The Hatred of the World

18 "If the world hates you, know that it has hated me before it hated you. **19** If you were of the world, the world would love you as its own; but because you are not of the world, but I chose you out of the world, therefore the world hates you. **20** Remember the word that I said to you: 'A servant is not greater than his master.' If they persecuted me, they will also persecute you. If they kept my word, they will also keep yours. **21** But all these things they will do to you on account of my name, because they do not know him who sent me. **22** If I had not come and spoken to them, they would not have been guilty of sin,[3] but now they have no excuse for their sin. **23** Whoever hates me hates my Father also. **24** If I had not done among them the works that no one else did, they would not be guilty of sin, but now they have seen and hated both me and my Father. **25** But the word that is written in their Law must be fulfilled: 'They hated me without a cause.'

26 "But when the Helper comes, whom I will send to you from the Father, the Spirit of truth, who proceeds from the Father, he will bear witness about me. **27** And you also will bear witness, because you have been with me from the beginning.

> **FACT**
>
> Sadly, many people despise and hate Christians, but this is a reflection of the world's attitude toward Christ, as Christians live their lives for Christ.

---

3.   Greek *they would not have sin*; also verse 24.

16 "I have said all these things to you to keep you from falling away. ² They will put you out of the synagogues. Indeed, the hour is coming when whoever kills you will think he is offering service to God. ³ And they will do these things because they have not known the Father, nor me. ⁴ But I have said these things to you, that when their hour comes you may remember that I told them to you.

The Work of the Holy Spirit

Regarding verse 2, this is exactly what Saul (who was later named Paul) was doing before he was saved. Paul is the Author of Romans, the next book in *Begin*.

"I did not say these things to you from the beginning, because I was with you. ⁵ But now I am going to him who sent me, and none of you asks me, 'Where are you going?' ⁶ But because I have said these things to you, sorrow has filled your heart. ⁷ Nevertheless, I tell you the truth: it is to your advantage that I go away, for if I do not go away, the Helper will not come to you. But if I go, I will send him to you. ⁸ And when he comes, he will convict the world concerning sin and righteousness and judgment: ⁹ concerning sin, because they do not believe in me; ¹⁰ concerning righteousness, because I go to the Father, and you will see me no longer; ¹¹ concerning judgment, because the ruler of this world is judged.

¹² "I still have many things to say to you, but you cannot bear them now. ¹³ When the Spirit of truth comes, he will guide you into all the truth, for he will not speak on his own authority, but whatever he hears he will speak, and he will declare to you the things that are to come. ¹⁴ He will glorify me, for he will take what is mine and declare it to you. ¹⁵ All that the Father has is mine; therefore I said that he will take what is mine and declare it to you.

Your Sorrow Will Turn into Joy

16 "A little while, and you will see me no longer; and again a little while, and you will see me." **17** So some of his disciples said to one another, "What is this that he says to us, 'A little while, and you will not see me, and again a little while, and you will see me'; and, 'because I am going to the Father'?" **18** So they were saying, "What does he mean by 'a little while'? We do not know what he is talking about." **19** Jesus knew that they wanted to ask him, so he said to them, "Is this what you are asking yourselves, what I meant by saying, 'A little while and you will not see me, and again a little while and you will see me'? **20** Truly, truly, I say to you, you will weep and lament, but the world will rejoice. You will be sorrowful, but your sorrow will turn into joy. **21** When a woman is giving birth, she has sorrow because her hour has come, but when she has delivered the baby, she no longer remembers the anguish, for joy that a human being has been born into the world. **22** So also you have sorrow now, but I will see you again, and your hearts will rejoice, and no one will take your joy from you. **23** In that day you will ask nothing of me. Truly, truly, I say to you, whatever you ask of the Father in my name, he will give it to you. **24** Until now you have asked nothing in my name. Ask, and you will receive, that your joy may be full.

Did you know Jesus repeatedly prophesied about coming back to life? Unlike all other religious leaders, Christ proved He had power over death.

I Have Overcome the World

25 "I have said these things to you in figures of speech. The hour is coming when I will no longer speak to you in figures of speech but will tell you plainly about the

Father. **26**In that day you will ask in my name, and I do not say to you that I will ask the Father on your behalf; **27**for the Father himself loves you, because you have loved me and have believed that I came from God.[1] **28**I came from the Father and have come into the world, and now I am leaving the world and going to the Father."

29 His disciples said, "Ah, now you are speaking plainly and not using figurative speech! **30** Now we know that you know all things and do not need anyone to question you; this is why we believe that you came from God." **31** Jesus answered them, "Do you now believe? **32**Behold, the hour is coming, indeed it has come, when you will be scattered, each to his own home, and will leave me alone. Yet I am not alone, for the Father is with me. **33**I have said these things to you, that in me you may have peace. In the world you will have tribulation. But take heart; I have overcome the world."

cross-ref

Romans 8:5

See page 166

---

1.   Some manuscripts *from the Father.*

Just because someone becomes a Christian doesn't mean they are perfect. Christians still fall short. Sometimes people meet a Christian who wrongs them, but they should not blame Christ. Even these Christians are still learning.

For to this end we toil and strive, because we have our hope set on the living God, who is the Savior of all people, especially of those who believe (1 Timothy 4:10).

The High Priestly Prayer

17 When Jesus had spoken these words, he lifted up his eyes to heaven, and said, "Father, the hour has come; glorify your Son that the Son may glorify you, 2 since you have given him authority over all flesh, to give eternal life to all whom you have given him. 3 And this is eternal life, that they know you the only true God, and Jesus Christ whom you have sent. 4 I glorified you on earth, having accomplished the work that you gave me to do. 5 And now, Father, glorify me in your own presence with the glory that I had with you before the world existed. 6 "I have manifested your name to the people whom you gave me out of the world. Yours they were, and you gave them to me, and they have kept your word. 7 Now they know that everything that you have given me is from you. 8 For I have given them the words that you gave me, and they have received them and have come to know in truth that I came from you; and they have believed that you sent me. 9 I am praying for them. I am not praying for the world but for those whom you have given me, for they are yours. 10 All mine are yours, and yours are mine, and I am glorified in them. 11 And I am no longer in the world, but they are in the world, and I am coming to you. Holy Father, keep them in your name, which you have given me, that they may be one, even as we are one. 12 While I was with them, I kept them in your name, which you have given me. I have guarded them, and not one of them has been lost except the son of destruction, that the Scripture might be fulfilled. 13 But now I am coming to you, and these things I speak in the world, that they may have my joy fulfilled in

FACT

John 17 records an incredible prayer from God the Son to God the Father.

themselves. **14** I have given them your word, and the world has hated them because they are not of the world, just as I am not of the world. **15** I do not ask that you take them out of the world, but that you keep them from the evil one.¹ **16** They are not of the world, just as I am not of the world. **17** Sanctify them² in the truth; your word is truth. **18** As you sent me into the world, so I have sent them into the world. **19** And for their sake I consecrate myself,³ that they also may be sanctified⁴ in truth.

20 "I do not ask for these only, but also for those who will believe in me through their word, **21** that they may all be one, just as you, Father, are in me, and I in you, that they also may be in us, so that the world may believe that you have sent me. **22** The glory that you have given me I have given to them, that they may be one even as we are one, **23** I in them and you in me, that they may become perfectly one, so that the world may know that you sent me and loved them even as you loved me. **24** Father, I desire that they also, whom you have given me, may be with me where I am, to see my glory that you have given me because you loved me before the foundation of the world. **25** O righteous Father, even though the world does not know you, I know you, and these know that you have sent me. **26** I made known to them your name, and I will continue to make it known, that the love with which you have loved me may be in them, and I in them."

Did you realize that Jesus' prayer included us?

---

1. Or *from evil.*
2. Greek *Set them apart* (for holy service to God).
3. Or *I sanctify myself; or I set myself apart* (for holy service to God).
4. Greek *may be set apart* (for holy service to God).

Betrayal and Arrest of Jesus

18 When Jesus had spoken these words, he went out with his disciples across the brook Kidron, where there was a garden, which he and his disciples entered. **2** Now Judas, who betrayed him, also knew the place, for Jesus often met there with his disciples. **3** So Judas, having procured a band of soldiers and some officers from the chief priests and the Pharisees, went there with lanterns and torches and weapons. **4** Then Jesus, knowing all that would happen to him, came forward and said to them, "Whom do you seek?" **5** They answered him, "Jesus of Nazareth." Jesus said to them, "I am he."[1] Judas, who betrayed him, was standing with them. **6** When Jesus[2] said to them, "I am he," they drew back and fell to the ground. **7** So he asked them again, "Whom do you seek?" And they said, "Jesus of Nazareth." **8** Jesus answered, "I told you that I am he. So, if you seek me, let these men go." **9** This was to fulfill the word that he had spoken: "Of those whom you gave me I have lost not one." **10** Then Simon Peter, having a sword, drew it and struck the high priest's servant[3] and cut off his right ear. (The servant's name was Malchus.) **11** So Jesus said to Peter, "Put your sword into its sheath; shall I not drink the cup that the Father has given me?"

cross-ref

But Jesus said, "No more of this!" And he touched his ear and healed him (Luke 22:51).

Jesus Faces Annas and Caiaphas

12 So the band of soldiers and their captain and the officers of the Jews[4] arrested Jesus and bound

---

1. Greek *I am*; also verses 6, 8.
2. Greek *he*.
3. Greek *bondservant*; twice in this verse.
4. Greek *Ioudaioi* probably refers here to Jewish religious leaders, and others under their influence, in that time; also verses 14, 31, 36, 38.

him. **13** First they led him to Annas, for he was the father-in-law of Caiaphas, who was high priest that year. **14** It was Caiaphas who had advised the Jews that it would be expedient that one man should die for the people.

Peter Denies Jesus

15 Simon Peter followed Jesus, and so did another disciple. Since that disciple was known to the high priest, he entered with Jesus into the courtyard of the high priest, **16** but Peter stood outside at the door. So the other disciple, who was known to the high priest, went out and spoke to the servant girl who kept watch at the door, and brought Peter in. **17** The servant girl at the door said to Peter, "You also are not one of this man's disciples, are you?" He said, "I am not." **18** Now the servants[5] and officers had made a charcoal fire, because it was cold, and they were standing and warming themselves. Peter also was with them, standing and warming himself.

The High Priest Questions Jesus

19 The high priest then questioned Jesus about his disciples and his teaching. **20** Jesus answered him, "I have spoken openly to the world. I have always taught in synagogues and in the temple, where all Jews come together. I have said nothing in secret. **21** Why do you ask me? Ask those who have heard me what I said to them; they know what I said." **22** When he had said these things, one of the

> **FACT**
>
> The high priests were basically the highest religious authority for the Jews.

---

5. Greek *bondservants*; also verse 26.

officers standing by struck Jesus with his hand, saying, "Is that how you answer the high priest?" 23 Jesus answered him, "If what I said is wrong, bear witness about the wrong; but if what I said is right, why do you strike me?" 24 Annas then sent him bound to Caiaphas the high priest.

Peter Denies Jesus Again

Jesus said, "I tell you, Peter, the rooster will not crow this day, until you deny three times that you know me" (Luke 22:34).

25 Now Simon Peter was standing and warming himself. So they said to him, "You also are not one of his disciples, are you?" He denied it and said, "I am not." 26 One of the servants of the high priest, a relative of the man whose ear Peter had cut off, asked, "Did I not see you in the garden with him?" 27 Peter again denied it, and at once a rooster crowed.

Jesus Before Pilate

28 Then they led Jesus from the house of Caiaphas to the governor's headquarters.[6] It was early morning. They themselves did not enter the governor's headquarters, so that they would not be defiled, but could eat the Passover. 29 So Pilate went outside to them and said, "What accusation do you bring against this man?" 30 They answered him, "If this man were not doing evil, we would not have delivered him over to you." 31 Pilate said to them, "Take him yourselves and judge him by your own law." The Jews said to him, "It is not lawful for us to put anyone to death." 32 This was to fulfill the word that Jesus had spoken to show by what kind of death he was going to die.

---

6. Greek *the praetorium.*

cross-ref

My Kingdom Is Not of This World

33 So Pilate entered his headquarters again and called Jesus and said to him, "Are you the King of the Jews?" **34** Jesus answered, "Do you say this of your own accord, or did others say it to you about me?" **35** Pilate answered, "Am I a Jew? Your own nation and the chief priests have delivered you over to me. What have you done?" **36** Jesus answered, "My kingdom is not of this world. If my kingdom were of this world, my servants would have been fighting, that I might not be delivered over to the Jews. But my kingdom is not from the world." **37** Then Pilate said to him, "So you are a king?" Jesus answered, "You say that I am a king. For this purpose I was born and for this purpose I have come into the world — to bear witness to the truth. Everyone who is of the truth listens to my voice." **38** Pilate said to him, "What is truth?"

After he had said this, he went back outside to the Jews and told them, "I find no guilt in him. **39** But you have a custom that I should release one man for you at the Passover. So do you want me to release to you the King of the Jews?" **40** They cried out again, "Not this man, but Barabbas!" Now Barabbas was a robber.⁷

Jesus is the truth (John 14:6) and Pilate asked, "What is truth?" while looking truth in the eye!

---

7. *Or an insurrectionist.*

Jesus Delivered to Be Crucified

19 Then Pilate took Jesus and flogged him. ² And the soldiers twisted together a crown of thorns and put it on his head and arrayed him in a purple robe. ³ They came up to him, saying, "Hail, King of the Jews!" and struck him with their hands. ⁴ Pilate went out again and said to them, "See, I am bringing him out to you that you may know that I find no guilt in him." ⁵ So Jesus came out, wearing the crown of thorns and the purple robe. Pilate said to them, "Behold the man!" ⁶ When the chief priests and the officers saw him, they cried out, "Crucify him, crucify him!" Pilate said to them, "Take him yourselves and crucify him, for I find no guilt in him." ⁷ The Jews[1] answered him, "We have a law, and according to that law he ought to die because he has made himself the Son of God." ⁸ When Pilate heard this statement, he was even more afraid. ⁹ He entered his headquarters again and said to Jesus, "Where are you from?" But Jesus gave him no answer. ¹⁰ So Pilate said to him, "You will not speak to me? Do you not know that I have authority to release you and authority to crucify you?" ¹¹ Jesus answered him, "You would have no authority over me at all unless it had been given you from above. Therefore he who delivered me over to you has the greater sin." ¹² From then on Pilate sought to release him, but the Jews cried out, "If you release this man, you are not Caesar's friend. Everyone who makes himself a king opposes Caesar." ¹³ So when Pilate heard these words, he brought Jesus

FACT

When the Jews cried out that they had no king but Caesar, they revealed that God was not their King. They sided with human authority over the Son of God.

---

1.   Greek *Ioudaioi* probably refers here to Jewish religious leaders, and others under their influence, in that time; also verses 12, 14, 31, 38.

out and sat down on the judgment seat at a place called The Stone Pavement, and in Aramaic[2] Gabbatha. [14] Now it was the day of Preparation of the Passover. It was about the sixth hour.[3] He said to the Jews, "Behold your King!" [15] They cried out, "Away with him, away with him, crucify him!" Pilate said to them, "Shall I crucify your King?" The chief priests answered, "We have no king but Caesar." [16] So he delivered him over to them to be crucified.

The Crucifixion

So they took Jesus, [17] and he went out, bearing his own cross, to the place called The Place of a Skull, which in Aramaic is called Golgotha. [18] There they crucified him, and with him two others, one on either side, and Jesus between them. [19] Pilate also wrote an inscription and put it on the cross. It read, "Jesus of Nazareth, the King of the Jews." [20] Many of the Jews read this inscription, for the place where Jesus was crucified was near the city, and it was written in Aramaic, in Latin, and in Greek. [21] So the chief priests of the Jews said to Pilate, "Do not write, 'The King of the Jews,' but rather, 'This man said, I am King of the Jews.' " [22] Pilate answered, "What I have written I have written."

[23] When the soldiers had crucified Jesus, they took his garments and divided them into four parts, one part for each soldier; also his tunic.[4] But the tunic was seamless, woven in one piece from top to bottom, [24] so they

> **cross-ref**
> Since the inscription was written in three different languages, we expect three slightly different wordings, and that is what we find in verse 19, Matthew 27:37, Mark 15:26 (a shortened version of one inscription), and Luke 23:38.

2. Or *Hebrew*; also verses 17, 20.
3. That is, about noon.
4. Greek *chiton*, a long garment worn under the cloak next to the skin.

said to one another, "Let us not tear it, but cast lots for it to see whose it shall be." This was to fulfill the Scripture which says,

"'They divided my garments among them,
and for my clothing they cast lots."

So the soldiers did these things, 25 but standing by the cross of Jesus were his mother and his mother's sister, Mary the wife of Clopas, and Mary Magdalene. 26 When Jesus saw his mother and the disciple whom he loved standing nearby, he said to his mother, "Woman, behold, your son!" 27 Then he said to the disciple, "Behold, your mother!" And from that hour the disciple took her to his own home.

cross-ref

"They divide my garments ..." was prophecy from a psalm of David many hundreds of years before (Psalm 22:18).

The Death of Jesus

28 After this, Jesus, knowing that all was now finished, said (to fulfill the Scripture), "I thirst." 29 A jar full of sour wine stood there, so they put a sponge full of the sour wine on a hyssop branch and held it to his mouth. 30 When Jesus had received the sour wine, he said, "It is finished," and he bowed his head and gave up his spirit.

Jesus' Side Is Pierced

31 Since it was the day of Preparation, and so that the bodies would not remain on the cross on the Sabbath (for that Sabbath was a high day), the Jews asked Pilate that their legs might be broken and that they might be taken away. 32 So the soldiers came and broke the legs of the first, and of the other who had

been crucified with him. **33** But when they came to Jesus and saw that he was already dead, they did not break his legs. **34** But one of the soldiers pierced his side with a spear, and at once there came out blood and water. **35** He who saw it has borne witness — his testimony is true, and he knows that he is telling the truth — that you also may believe. **36** For these things took place that the Scripture might be fulfilled: "Not one of his bones will be broken." **37** And again another Scripture says, "They will look on him whom they have pierced."

Jesus Is Buried

38 After these things Joseph of Arimathea, who was a disciple of Jesus, but secretly for fear of the Jews, asked Pilate that he might take away the body of Jesus, and Pilate gave him permission. So he came and took away his body. **39** Nicodemus also, who earlier had come to Jesus[5] by night, came bringing a mixture of myrrh and aloes, about seventy-five pounds[6] in weight. **40** So they took the body of Jesus and bound it in linen cloths with the spices, as is the burial custom of the Jews. **41** Now in the place where he was crucified there was a garden, and in the garden a new tomb in which no one had yet been laid. **42** So because of the Jewish day of Preparation, since the tomb was close at hand, they laid Jesus there.

Did you know Jesus was buried very close to the crucifixion site? They needed to bury Jesus quickly because it was preparation day before the Sabbath — when they were not allowed to do work.

---

5.   Greek *him*.
6.   Greek *one hundred litras*; a *litra* (or Roman pound) was equal to about 11 1/2 ounces or 327 grams.

The Resurrection

20 Now on the first day of the week Mary Magdalene came to the tomb early, while it was still dark, and saw that the stone had been taken away from the tomb. ² So she ran and went to Simon Peter and the other disciple, the one whom Jesus loved, and said to them, "They have taken the Lord out of the tomb, and we do not know where they have laid him." ³ So Peter went out with the other disciple, and they were going toward the tomb. ⁴ Both of them were running together, but the other disciple outran Peter and reached the tomb first. ⁵ And stooping to look in, he saw the linen cloths lying there, but he did not go in. ⁶ Then Simon Peter came, following him, and went into the tomb. He saw the linen cloths lying there, ⁷ and the face cloth, which had been on Jesus'¹ head, not lying with the linen cloths but folded up in a place by itself. ⁸ Then the other disciple, who had reached the tomb first, also went in, and he saw and believed; ⁹ for as yet they did not understand the Scripture, that he must rise from the dead. ¹⁰ Then the disciples went back to their homes.

FACT

At first they thought Jesus' body had been moved. It didn't dawn on them that Jesus had resurrected.

Jesus Appears to Mary Magdalene

¹¹ But Mary stood weeping outside the tomb, and as she wept she stooped to look into the tomb. ¹² And she saw two angels in white, sitting where the body of Jesus had lain, one at the head and one at the feet. ¹³ They said to her, "Woman, why are you weeping?" She said to them, "They have taken away my Lord, and

---

1. Greek *his*.

I do not know where they have laid him." **14** Having said this, she turned around and saw Jesus standing, but she did not know that it was Jesus. **15** Jesus said to her, "Woman, why are you weeping? Whom are you seeking?" Supposing him to be the gardener, she said to him, "Sir, if you have carried him away, tell me where you have laid him, and I will take him away." **16** Jesus said to her, "Mary." She turned and said to him in Aramaic,² "Rabboni!" (which means Teacher). **17** Jesus said to her, "Do not cling to me, for I have not yet ascended to the Father; but go to my brothers and say to them, 'I am ascending to my Father and your Father, to my God and your God.'" **18** Mary Magdalene went and announced to the disciples, "I have seen the Lord" — and that he had said these things to her.

Jesus Appears to the Disciples

19 On the evening of that day, the first day of the week, the doors being locked where the disciples were for fear of the Jews,³ Jesus came and stood among them and said to them, "Peace be with you." **20** When he had said this, he showed them his hands and his side. Then the disciples were glad when they saw the Lord. **21** Jesus said to them again, "Peace be with you. As the Father has sent me, even so I am sending you." **22** And when he had said this, he breathed on them and said to them, "Receive the Holy Spirit. **23** If you forgive the sins of any, they are forgiven them; if you withhold forgiveness from any, it is withheld."

> Can you imagine the surprise from the disciples when they realized Jesus was alive?

2. Or *Hebrew*.

3. Greek *Ioudaioi* probably refers here to Jewish religious leaders, and others under their influence, in that time.

Jesus and Thomas

24 Now Thomas, one of the Twelve, called the Twin,[4] was not with them when Jesus came. 25 So the other disciples told him, "We have seen the Lord." But he said to them, "Unless I see in his hands the mark of the nails, and place my finger into the mark of the nails, and place my hand into his side, I will never believe."

26 Eight days later, his disciples were inside again, and Thomas was with them. Although the doors were locked, Jesus came and stood among them and said, "Peace be with you." 27 Then he said to Thomas, "Put your finger here, and see my hands; and put out your hand, and place it in my side. Do not disbelieve, but believe." 28 Thomas answered him, "My Lord and my God!" 29 Jesus said to him, "Have you believed because you have seen me? Blessed are those who have not seen and yet have believed."

FACT

These events led to the nickname "Doubting Thomas."

The Purpose of This Book

30 Now Jesus did many other signs in the presence of the disciples, which are not written in this book; 31 but these are written so that you may believe that Jesus is the Christ, the Son of God, and that by believing you may have life in his name.

---

4.   Greek *Didymus*.

Some people today suggest Jesus didn't die, so when He appeared to everyone, it was no big deal. However, Jesus was up all night, beaten, flogged, forced to carry the "weapon of His death" to Golgotha, had a crown of thorns forced into His head, was hammered to a cross, was humiliated and endured false accusations, had His friend (Judas) betray Him and His discipes abandon Him, had a spear shoved through His side, and laid in a tomb until the third day. And yet, few who claim that Jesus didn't die would submit themselves to test this!

> Indeed, under the law almost everything is purified with blood, and without the shedding of blood there is no forgiveness of sins
> Hebrews 9:22

Jesus Appears to Seven Disciples

21 After this Jesus revealed himself again to the disciples by the Sea of Tiberias, and he revealed himself in this way. ²Simon Peter, Thomas (called the Twin), Nathanael of Cana in Galilee, the sons of Zebedee, and two others of his disciples were together. ³Simon Peter said to them, "I am going fishing." They said to him, "We will go with you." They went out and got into the boat, but that night they caught nothing. ⁴Just as day was breaking, Jesus stood on the shore; yet the disciples did not know that it was Jesus. ⁵Jesus said to them, "Children, do you have any fish?" They answered him, "No." ⁶He said to them, "Cast the net on the right side of the boat, and you will find some." So they cast it, and now they were not able to haul it in, because of the quantity of fish. ⁷That disciple whom Jesus loved therefore said to Peter, "It is the Lord!" When Simon Peter heard that it was the Lord, he put on his outer garment, for he was stripped for work, and threw himself into the sea. ⁸The other disciples came in the boat, dragging the net full of fish, for they were not far from the land, but about a hundred yards¹ off.

⁹When they got out on land, they saw a charcoal fire in place, with fish laid out on it, and bread. ¹⁰Jesus said to them, "Bring some of the fish that you have just caught." ¹¹So Simon Peter went aboard and hauled the net ashore, full of large fish, 153 of them. And although there were so many, the net was not torn. ¹²Jesus said to them, "Come and have breakfast." Now none of the

cross-ref

And he said to them, "Follow me, and I will make you fishers of men" (Matthew 4:19).

---

1. Greek *two hundred cubits*; a *cubit* was about 18 inches or 45 centimeters.

disciples dared ask him, "Who are you?" They knew it was the Lord. **13** Jesus came and took the bread and gave it to them, and so with the fish. **14** This was now the third time that Jesus was revealed to the disciples after he was raised from the dead.

Jesus and Peter

15 When they had finished breakfast, Jesus said to Simon Peter, "Simon, son of John, do you love me more than these?" He said to him, "Yes, Lord; you know that I love you." He said to him, "Feed my lambs." **16** He said to him a second time, "Simon, son of John, do you love me?" He said to him, "Yes, Lord; you know that I love you." He said to him, "Tend my sheep." **17** He said to him the third time, "Simon, son of John, do you love me?" Peter was grieved because he said to him the third time, "Do you love me?" and he said to him, "Lord, you know everything; you know that I love you." Jesus said to him, "Feed my sheep. **18** Truly, truly, I say to you, when you were young, you used to dress yourself and walk wherever you wanted, but when you are old, you will stretch out your hands, and another will dress you and carry you where you do not want to go." **19** (This he said to show by what kind of death he was to glorify God.) And after saying this he said to him, "Follow me."

> **Did you realize that Peter denied Jesus three times, and Jesus asked Peter three times if he loved Him?**

Jesus and the Beloved Apostle

20 Peter turned and saw the disciple whom Jesus loved following them, the one who also had leaned back against him during the supper and had said, "Lord, who is it that is going to betray you?" **21** When Peter saw him, he said to Jesus, "Lord, what about this man?" **22** Jesus said to him, "If it is my will that he remain until I come, what is that to you? You follow me!" **23** So the saying spread abroad among the brothers[2] that this disciple was not to die; yet Jesus did not say to him that he was not to die, but, "If it is my will that he remain until I come, what is that to you?"

24 This is the disciple who is bearing witness about these things, and who has written these things, and we know that his testimony is true.

25 Now there are also many other things that Jesus did. Were every one of them to be written, I suppose that the world itself could not contain the books that would be written.

FACT

There is so much more that could be said about what Jesus did, but what is written in the Bible is sufficient.

---

2. Or *brothers and sisters.*

Too often death is considered the final event in our lives. Without the hope for eternity in Christ, this life would be all we would experience. How has knowing about Christ's suffering and sacrifice on the Cross changed your perspective on not only this life, but an eternal life with Him?

Think about the people attending to Jesus' body after the crucifixion, and the ones Jesus revealed Himself to after having arisen. What does the Scripture reveal about them and their relationship to the Savior?

From the Ascension of Christ to Paul's Letter to the Romans

The period after Christ's ascension essentially begins the apostolic period. In the same way the prophets of the Old Testament spoke and wrote Scripture by means of the Holy Spirit, now Apostles were designated to do that (Luke 11:48–51).[1] Most of the Apostles were the Disciples of Christ (obviously excluding Judas, who betrayed Christ), but not all of them (Matthew 10:2–4).[2] And of course, not all Apostles were required to write a book, which was similar to the Old Testament prophets — some wrote and some didn't. The Bible reveals who the Apostles were:

1. Simon Peter (Matthew 10:2–4 for these first 12)
2. Andrew (Peter's brother)
3. James the son of Zebedee
4. John son of Zebedee and brother of James
5. Philip
6. Bartholomew
7. Thomas
8. Matthew the tax collector
9. James the son of Alphaeus
10. Lebbaeus Thaddaeus
11. Simon the Canaanite
12. ~~Judas Iscariot~~, who forfeited his right as an Apostle
13. Matthias (Acts 1:23–26)[3] Replaced Judas

1. Luke 11:48–51: So you are witnesses and you consent to the deeds of your fathers, for they killed them, and you build their tombs. Therefore also the Wisdom of God said, 'I will send them prophets and apostles, some of whom they will kill and persecute,' so that the blood of all the prophets, shed from the foundation of the world, may be charged against this generation, from the blood of Abel to the blood of Zechariah, who perished between the altar and the sanctuary. Yes, I tell you, it will be required of this generation.

2. Matthew 10:2–4: The names of the twelve apostles are these: first, Simon, who is called Peter, and Andrew his brother; James the son of Zebedee, and John his brother; Philip and Bartholomew; Thomas and Matthew the tax collector; James the son of Alphaeus, and Thaddaeus; Simon the Cananaean, and Judas Iscariot, who betrayed him.

3. Acts 1:23–26: And they put forward two, Joseph called Barsabbas, who was also called Justus, and Matthias. And they prayed and said, "You, Lord, who know the hearts of all, show which one of these two you have chosen to take the place in this ministry and apostleship from which Judas turned aside to go to his own place." And they cast lots for them, and the lot fell on Matthias, and he was numbered with the eleven apostles.

14. Paul (2 Corinthians 11:5,[4] 2 Corinthians 12:11–12,[5] etc.)
15. Barnabas (Acts 14:14)[6]
16. James the brother of Jesus (Galatians 1:19)[7]
17. Jesus is the Apostle (Hebrews 3:1)[8]

The Apostles account for any Scriptures after Christ. In other words, if it was not written or overseen by an Apostle, then it is not Scripture.[9] This would eliminate people who claim to be prophets of God after the apostolic period. In short, people like Muhammad, Joseph Smith, and others who claim to be prophets of God cannot be. And since many of their writings (Koran, Book of Mormon, etc.) are in contradiction with the Scriptures written by previous prophets and Apostles (Old and New Testaments), and God cannot deny Himself, then they cannot be from God.

During this time, though, the Apostles were starting churches and going about various missionary journeys preaching the Gospel and good news of Jesus and disciplining the early churches. It was at this time that Paul wrote a number of letters to various churches or Christians and other Apostles wrote letters as well. The Book of Romans is one penned by Paul, who was formerly Saul, a Jew who had been persecuting Christians severely before he was saved and granted apostleship by the Lord Jesus Christ.

---

4. 2 Corinthians 11:5: I [Paul] consider that I am not in the least inferior to these super-apostles.

5. 2 Corinthians 12:11–12: I [Paul] have been a fool! You forced me to it, for I ought to have been commended by you. For I was not at all inferior to these super-apostles, even though I am nothing. The signs of a true apostle were performed among you with utmost patience, with signs and wonders and mighty works.

6. Acts 14:14: But when the apostles Barnabas and Paul heard of it, they tore their garments and rushed out into the crowd, crying out,

7. Galatians 1:19: But I saw none of the other apostles except James the Lord's brother.

8. Hebrews 3:1: Therefore, holy brothers, you who share in a heavenly calling, consider Jesus, the apostle and high priest of our confession.

9. For example, *Hebrews* as per Hebrew 2:3 and early Church fathers Clement and Eusebius who said Paul was responsible for it, confirming 2 Peter 3:15–16; *Mark* by Peter and *Luke and Acts* by Paul as the early church fathers Irenaeus and Tertullian openly pointed out, and *Jude* by James as per Jude 1. For a more in-depth look at canon of Scripture see: http://www.answersingenesis.org/articles/aid/v3/n1/look-at-the-canon.

The Letter of Paul to the Romans

Greeting

1 Paul, a servant[1] of Christ Jesus, called to be an apostle, set apart for the gospel of God, **2** which he promised beforehand through his prophets in the holy Scriptures, **3** concerning his Son, who was descended from David[2] according to the flesh **4** and was declared to be the Son of God in power according to the Spirit of holiness by his resurrection from the dead, Jesus Christ our Lord, **5** through whom we have received grace and apostleship to bring about the obedience of faith for the sake of his name among all the nations, **6** including you who are called to belong to Jesus Christ, **7** To all those in Rome who are loved by God and called to be saints:

Grace to you and peace from God our Father and the Lord Jesus Christ.

Longing to Go to Rome

8 First, I thank my God through Jesus Christ for all of you, because your faith is proclaimed in all the world. **9** For God is my witness, whom I serve with my spirit in the gospel of his Son, that without ceasing I mention you **10** always in my prayers, asking that somehow by God's will I may now at last succeed in coming to you. **11** For I long to see you, that I may impart to you some spiritual gift to strengthen you — **12** that is, that we may be

FACT

Paul was very hostile to Christians prior to getting saved.

1. Or *slave*.
2. Or *who came from the offspring of David*.

mutually encouraged by each other's faith, both yours and mine. [13] I do not want you to be unaware, brothers,[3] that I have often intended to come to you (but thus far have been prevented), in order that I may reap some harvest among you as well as among the rest of the Gentiles. [14] I am under obligation both to Greeks and to barbarians,[4] both to the wise and to the foolish. [15] So I am eager to preach the gospel to you also who are in Rome.

The Righteous Shall Live by Faith

[16] For I am not ashamed of the gospel, for it is the power of God for salvation to everyone who believes, to the Jew first and also to the Greek. [17] For in it the righteousness of God is revealed from faith for faith,[5] as it is written, "The righteous shall live by faith."[6]

God's Wrath on Unrighteousness

[18] For the wrath of God is revealed from heaven against all ungodliness and unrighteousness of men, who by their unrighteousness suppress the truth. [19] For what can be known about God is plain to them, because God has shown it to them. [20] For his invisible attributes, namely, his eternal power and divine nature, have been clearly perceived, ever since the creation of the world,[7] in the things that have been made. So they are without excuse. [21] For although they

FACT

God points out that all people know He exists, but suppress this knowledge — so they are without excuse when judgment comes.

---

3. Or *brothers and sisters*. The plural Greek word *adelphoi* (translated "brothers") refers to siblings in a family. In New Testament usage, depending on the context, *adelphoi* may refer either to men or to both men and women who are siblings (brothers and sisters) in God's family, the church.

4. That is, non-Greeks.

5. Or *beginning and ending in faith*.

6. Or *The one who by faith is righteous shall live*.

7. Or *clearly perceived from the creation of the world*.

knew God, they did not honor him as God or give thanks to him, but they became futile in their thinking, and their foolish hearts were darkened. ²²Claiming to be wise, they became fools, ²³and exchanged the glory of the immortal God for images resembling mortal man and birds and animals and creeping things.

²⁴Therefore God gave them up in the lusts of their hearts to impurity, to the dishonoring of their bodies among themselves, ²⁵because they exchanged the truth about God for a lie and worshiped and served the creature rather than the Creator, who is blessed forever! Amen.

FACT

This description in Romans 1 aptly describes today's culture — both the moral issues and exchanging truth for a lie (evolution).

²⁶For this reason God gave them up to dishonorable passions. For their women exchanged natural relations for those that are contrary to nature; ²⁷and the men likewise gave up natural relations with women and were consumed with passion for one another, men committing shameless acts with men and receiving in themselves the due penalty for their error.

²⁸And since they did not see fit to acknowledge God, God gave them up to a debased mind to do what ought not to be done. ²⁹They were filled with all manner of unrighteousness, evil, covetousness, malice. They are full of envy, murder, strife, deceit, maliciousness. They are gossips, ³⁰slanderers, haters of God, insolent, haughty, boastful, inventors of evil, disobedient to parents, ³¹foolish, faithless, heartless, ruthless. ³²Though they know God's righteous decree that those who practice such things deserve to die, they not only do them but give approval to those who practice them.

Did you notice how Paul pointed out that people would give glory, not to God, but to images resembling mortal man, birds, animals, and creeping things? Many cultures have done this worshiping things that are half-human and half-animal (think of something like "centaur" which is half human and half horse). But today's variation has apelike creatures that are half-men and half-ape — but notice these are just images, not reality. But our evolutionary culture buys into this lie today and uses it as a vice to reject Christ.

Be watchful, stand firm in the faith, act like men, be strong (1 Corinthians 16:13).

God's Righteous Judgment

2 Therefore you have no excuse, O man, every one of you who judges. For in passing judgment on another you condemn yourself, because you, the judge, practice the very same things. ² We know that the judgment of God rightly falls on those who practice such things. ³ Do you suppose, O man — you who judge those who practice such things and yet do them yourself — that you will escape the judgment of God? ⁴ Or do you presume on the riches of his kindness and forbearance and patience, not knowing that God's kindness is meant to lead you to repentance? ⁵ But because of your hard and impenitent heart you are storing up wrath for yourself on the day of wrath when God's righteous judgment will be revealed. ⁶ He will render to each one according to his works: ⁷ to those who by patience in well-doing seek for glory and honor and immortality, he will give eternal life; ⁸ but for those who are self-seeking¹ and do not obey the truth, but obey unrighteousness, there will be wrath and fury. ⁹ There will be tribulation and distress for every human being who does evil, the Jew first and also the Greek, ¹⁰ but glory and honor and peace for everyone who does good, the Jew first and also the Greek. ¹¹ For God shows no partiality.

God's Judgment and the Law

¹² For all who have sinned without the law will also perish without the law, and all who have sinned under the law will be judged by the law. ¹³ For it is not the

---

cross-ref

There is neither Jew nor Greek, there is neither slave nor free, there is neither male nor female, for you are all one in Christ Jesus (Galatians 3:28).

---

1. Or *contentious*.

hearers of the law who are righteous before God, but the doers of the law who will be justified. **14** For when Gentiles, who do not have the law, by nature do what the law requires, they are a law to themselves, even though they do not have the law. **15** They show that the work of the law is written on their hearts, while their conscience also bears witness, and their conflicting thoughts accuse or even excuse them **16** on that day when, according to my gospel, God judges the secrets of men by Christ Jesus.

17 But if you call yourself a Jew and rely on the law and boast in God **18** and know his will and approve what is excellent, because you are instructed from the law; **19** and if you are sure that you yourself are a guide to the blind, a light to those who are in darkness, **20** an instructor of the foolish, a teacher of children, having in the law the embodiment of knowledge and truth — **21** you then who teach others, do you not teach yourself? While you preach against stealing, do you steal? **22** You who say that one must not commit adultery, do you commit adultery? You who abhor idols, do you rob temples? **23** You who boast in the law dishonor God by breaking the law. **24** For, as it is written, "The name of God is blasphemed among the Gentiles because of you."

25 For circumcision indeed is of value if you obey the law, but if you break the law, your circumcision becomes uncircumcision. **26** So, if a man who is uncircumcised keeps the precepts of the law, will not his uncircumcision be regarded[2] as circumcision? **27** Then

> **FACT**
>
> Circumcision goes back to the covenant with Abraham — the father of the Jews (and many Arabs through Ishmael and Edomites through Esau).

---

2. Or *counted*.

he who is physically[3] uncircumcised but keeps the law will condemn you who have the written code[4] and circumcision but break the law. **28** For no one is a Jew who is merely one outwardly, nor is circumcision outward and physical. **29** But a Jew is one inwardly, and circumcision is a matter of the heart, by the Spirit, not by the letter. His praise is not from man but from God.

Does Paul point out that true circumcision is of the body or of the heart?

---

3. Or *is by nature.*
4. Or *the letter.*

Did you know that it was the Lord who instructed Paul to witness in Rome? From this point on, Paul did as the Lord commanded. Church fathers point out that Paul was beheaded in Rome by Nero, a ruthless Roman emperor.

The following night the Lord stood by him and said, "Take courage, for as you have testified to the facts about me in Jerusalem, so you must testify also in Rome" (Acts 23:11).

God's Righteousness Upheld

3 Then what advantage has the Jew? Or what is the value of circumcision? ² Much in every way. To begin with, the Jews were entrusted with the oracles of God. ³ What if some were unfaithful? Does their faithlessness nullify the faithfulness of God? ⁴ By no means! Let God be true though every one were a liar, as it is written, "That you may be justified in your words, and prevail when you are judged."

⁵ But if our unrighteousness serves to show the righteousness of God, what shall we say? That God is unrighteous to inflict wrath on us? (I speak in a human way.) ⁶ By no means! For then how could God judge the world? ⁷ But if through my lie God's truth abounds to his glory, why am I still being condemned as a sinner? ⁸ And why not do evil that good may come? — as some people slanderously charge us with saying. Their condemnation is just.

No One Is Righteous

⁹ What then? Are we Jews¹ any better off?² No, not at all. For we have already charged that all, both Jews and Greeks, are under sin, ¹⁰ as it is written:

> "None is righteous, no, not one; ¹¹ no one understands; no one seeks for God. ¹² All have turned aside; together they have become worthless; no one does good, not even one.
> ¹³ "Their throat is an open grave; they use their tongues to deceive. The venom of asps is under their lips."
> ¹⁴ Their mouth is full of curses and bitterness.

FACT

Paul continually says to be just, putting aside evil, unrighteousness, and lying.

---

1. Greek *Are we.*
2. Or *at any disadvantage?*

15 "Their feet are swift to shed blood; **16** in their paths are ruin and misery, **17** and the way of peace they have not known. **18** There is no fear of God before their eyes."

19 Now we know that whatever the law says it speaks to those who are under the law, so that every mouth may be stopped, and the whole world may be held accountable to God. **20** For by works of the law no human being[3] will be justified in his sight, since through the law comes knowledge of sin.

The Righteousness of God Through Faith

21 But now the righteousness of God has been manifested apart from the law, although the Law and the Prophets bear witness to it — **22** the righteousness of God through faith in Jesus Christ for all who believe. For there is no distinction: **23** for all have sinned and fall short of the glory of God, **24** and are justified by his grace as a gift, through the redemption that is in Christ Jesus, **25** whom God put forward as a propitiation by his blood, to be received by faith. This was to show God's righteousness, because in his divine forbearance he had passed over former sins. **26** It was to show his righteousness at the present time, so that he might be just and the justifier of the one who has faith in Jesus.

27 Then what becomes of our boasting? It is excluded. By what kind of law? By a law of works? No, but by the law of faith. **28** For we hold that one is justified by faith apart from works of the law. **29** Or is God the God of Jews only? Is he not the God of Gentiles also? Yes, of Gentiles also, **30** since God is one — who will justify the circumcised by faith and the uncircumcised through faith. **31** Do we then overthrow the law by this faith? By no means! On the contrary, we uphold the law.

> Did you know that most religions are "works" based, whereas Christianity is based on "grace"? Grace is freely offered because God did the work for us! We do works because of God's grace, not to try to "earn" salvation, but as a result of salvation.

---

3. Greek *flesh.*

Abraham Justified by Faith

4 What then shall we say was gained by[1] Abraham, our forefather according to the flesh? **2** For if Abraham was justified by works, he has something to boast about, but not before God. **3** For what does the Scripture say? "Abraham believed God, and it was counted to him as righteousness." **4** Now to the one who works, his wages are not counted as a gift but as his due. **5** And to the one who does not work but believes in[2] him who justifies the ungodly, his faith is counted as righteousness, **6** just as David also speaks of the blessing of the one to whom God counts righteousness apart from works:

> **7** "Blessed are those whose lawless deeds are forgiven, and whose sins are covered;
> **8** blessed is the man against whom the Lord will not count his sin."

9 Is this blessing then only for the circumcised, or also for the uncircumcised? For we say that faith was counted to Abraham as righteousness. **10** How then was it counted to him? Was it before or after he had been circumcised? It was not after, but before he was circumcised. **11** He received the sign of circumcision as a seal of the righteousness that he had by faith while he was still uncircumcised. The purpose was to make him the father of all who believe without being circumcised, so that righteousness would be

---

cross-ref

By faith Abraham obeyed when he was called to go out to a place. . . . By faith Abraham, when he was tested, offered up Isaac, and he who had received the promises was in the act of offering up his only son (Hebrews 11:8a, 17).

---

1. Some manuscripts *say about*.
2. Or *but trusts*; compare verse 24.

counted to them as well, **12** and to make him the father of the circumcised who are not merely circumcised but who also walk in the footsteps of the faith that our father Abraham had before he was circumcised.

The Promise Realized Through Faith

13 For the promise to Abraham and his offspring that he would be heir of the world did not come through the law but through the righteousness of faith. **14** For if it is the adherents of the law who are to be the heirs, faith is null and the promise is void. **15** For the law brings wrath, but where there is no law there is no transgression.

16 That is why it depends on faith, in order that the promise may rest on grace and be guaranteed to all his offspring — not only to the adherent of the law but also to the one who shares the faith of Abraham, who is the father of us all, **17** as it is written, "I have made you the father of many nations" — in the presence of the God in whom he believed, who gives life to the dead and calls into existence the things that do not exist. **18** In hope he believed against hope, that he should become the father of many nations, as he had been told, "So shall your offspring be." **19** He did not weaken in faith when he considered his own body, which was as good as dead (since he was about a hundred years old), or when he considered the barrenness³ of Sarah's womb. **20** No unbelief made him waver concerning the prom-

> **cross-ref**
>
> So then, the law was our guardian until Christ came, in order that we might be justified by faith (Galatians 3:24).

---

3. Greek *deadness*.

ise of God, but he grew strong in his faith as he gave glory to God, **21** fully convinced that God was able to do what he had promised. **22** That is why his faith was "counted to him as righteousness." **23** But the words "it was counted to him" were not written for his sake alone, **24** but for ours also. It will be counted to us who believe in him who raised from the dead Jesus our Lord, **25** who was delivered up for our trespasses and raised for our justification.

Jesus . . . said to them, "Those who are well have no need of a physician, but those who are sick. I came not to call the righteous, but sinners" (Mark 2:17).

There have been "big" words used up to this point, so let's take some time to define them:

Justification: to be declared innocent; acquitted

Sanctification: the action of being set apart as holy

Salvation: being delivered from the punishment for sin, which is death, ultimately an eternal death

Grace: the free and unmerited favor of God toward man

For by grace you have been saved through faith. And this is not your own doing; it is the gift of God (Ephesians 2:8).

Why Don't Christians Follow all the Old Testament Laws?

Have you ever heard the claim that Christians are living contradictions because they don't follow all the Old Testament laws (e.g., offering sin offerings, Leviticus 5:5–6)? The answer is simple and yet overlooked by non-Christians who have not read or at least fail to understand some basic theology.

The way Christians look at Old Testament Law is primarily based on one of two theologies[1] — either dispensational theology or covenant theology. Both agree that when a new covenant came about, rules changed. Some of these covenants are the original Edenic (inferred), Noahic, Mosaic, and now the new one in Christ's blood.

For an overview example, from the Edenic covenant, man was vegetarian (Genesis 1:30). When there was a new covenant with Noah, man was allowed to eat clean and unclean meat (Genesis 9:3). With Moses and the covenant with the Israelites, it was even more strict, limiting them to eat only meat that was clean (Leviticus 11:47, etc.). In the new covenant with Christ's blood, this was again opened up (Romans 14:1–4).[2] And in heaven, we will be vegetarian again to complete the cycle (there will be no death in heaven [Revelation 21:4], so no meat will be available).

Food Permitted to be Eaten

Edenic — vegetarian

Noahic — vegetarian foods, clean and unclean meats

Mosaic — vegetarian foods, clean meats

---

1. In rare cases, some other Christians hold to views different from these two, but to answer this alleged contradiction I am going to stick to the main two theologies that Christians adhere to. So please forgive me if I have not dived into one of the other theological positions.

2. There were some who still preferred to utilize diets different from this in Scripture. For example, Daniel in the Mosaic covenant used the vegetarian diet of Genesis 1:30 instead of eating the pagan sacrificed meats while in captivity, so this was not a sin. In the New Covenant, some who were weak ate only vegetables, according to Paul in Romans 14:2, though of course there were those with health issues, too. Keep in mind that like Daniel this was *not sinful*, but merely a sign of weakness.

New Covenant in Christ — vegetarian foods, clean and
    unclean meats
Heaven — vegetarian

So God's rules *to man* can change at various covenants (but God's character has never changed). With regard to various other laws, there are also some changes, but it may not be as "cut and dried" as the example above. These two views differ in the way they look at *how* the laws change. In essence they say:

Covenant theology: *rules apply unless done away with in the next covenant.* In other words, each covenant is seen as part of a greater covenant that now has modifications.

Dispensational theology: *previous rules don't apply in a new covenant unless reiterated in the next covenant.* In other words, new dispensations do away with each previous rule in previous covenants when they are fulfilled and new rules need to be stated.

Both of these affect the way that Old Testament laws are viewed. Both sides agree on most laws because so much was reiterated in the New Testament and changed in the New Testament.[3] But some things went away — obviously the sacrificial stuff such as Levitius 5:5–6, which Christ fulfilled. But with either of these theologies it answers why Christians do not adhere to all the Old Testament laws.

With this issue, both sides view the Bible as the authoritative Word of God. If you are interested in pursuing these theologies in more detail, I suggest you contact your local denomination to see which view your church holds to and get into the finer details of it. They should be able to fill you in on the details of that position.

---

3. Where they disagree is where it gets interesting, such as bestiality, tattoos, etc.

Peace with God Through Faith

5 Therefore, since we have been justified by faith, we[1] have peace with God through our Lord Jesus Christ. [2] Through him we have also obtained access by faith[2] into this grace in which we stand, and we[3] rejoice[4] in hope of the glory of God. [3] Not only that, but we rejoice in our sufferings, knowing that suffering produces endurance, [4] and endurance produces character, and character produces hope, [5] and hope does not put us to shame, because God's love has been poured into our hearts through the Holy Spirit who has been given to us. [6] For while we were still weak, at the right time Christ died for the ungodly. [7] For one will scarcely die for a righteous person — though perhaps for a good person one would dare even to die — [8] but God shows his love for us in that while we were still sinners, Christ died for us. [9] Since, therefore, we have now been justified by his blood, much more shall we be saved by him from the wrath of God. [10] For if while we were enemies we were reconciled to God by the death of his Son, much more, now that we are reconciled, shall we be saved by his life. [11] More than that, we also rejoice in God through our Lord Jesus Christ, through whom we have now received reconciliation.

> "But God shows his love for us in that while we were still sinners, Christ died for us" (Romans 5:8).

Death in Adam, Life in Christ

[12] Therefore, just as sin came into the world through one man, and death through sin, and so death spread to

---

1. Some manuscripts *let us*.
2. Some manuscripts omit *by faith*.
3. Or *let us*; also verse 3.
4. Or *boast*; also verses 3, 11.

all men[5] because all sinned — **13** for sin indeed was in the world before the law was given, but sin is not counted where there is no law. **14** Yet death reigned from Adam to Moses, even over those whose sinning was not like the transgression of Adam, who was a type of the one who was to come.

15 But the free gift is not like the trespass. For if many died through one man's trespass, much more have the grace of God and the free gift by the grace of that one man Jesus Christ abounded for many. **16** And the free gift is not like the result of that one man's sin. For the judgment following one trespass brought condemnation, but the free gift following many trespasses brought justification. **17** For if, because of one man's trespass, death reigned through that one man, much more will those who receive the abundance of grace and the free gift of righteousness reign in life through the one man Jesus Christ.

18 Therefore, as one trespass[6] led to condemnation for all men, so one act of righteousness[7] leads to justification and life for all men. **19** For as by the one man's disobedience the many were made sinners, so by the one man's obedience the many will be made righteous. **20** Now the law came in to increase the trespass, but where sin increased, grace abounded all the more, **21** so that, as sin reigned in death, grace also might reign through righteousness leading to eternal life through Jesus Christ our Lord.

> **cross-ref**
>
> And through him [Christ] to reconcile to himself all things, whether on earth or in heaven, making peace by the blood of his cross (Colossians 1:20).

---

5. The Greek word *anthropoi* refers here to both men and women; also twice in verse 18.

6. Or *the trespass of one*.

7. Or *the act of righteousness of one*.

Dead to Sin, Alive to God

6 What shall we say then? Are we to continue in sin that grace may abound? **2** By no means! How can we who died to sin still live in it? **3** Do you not know that all of us who have been baptized into Christ Jesus were baptized into his death? **4** We were buried therefore with him by baptism into death, in order that, just as Christ was raised from the dead by the glory of the Father, we too might walk in newness of life. **5** For if we have been united with him in a death like his, we shall certainly be united with him in a resurrection like his. **6** We know that our old self[1] was crucified with him in order that the body of sin might be brought to nothing, so that we would no longer be enslaved to sin. **7** For one who has died has been set free[2] from sin. **8** Now if we have died with Christ, we believe that we will also live with him. **9** We know that Christ, being raised from the dead, will never die again; death no longer has dominion over him. **10** For the death he died he died to sin, once for all, but the life he lives he lives to God. **11** So you also must consider yourselves dead to sin and alive to God in Christ Jesus.

12 Let not sin therefore reign in your mortal body, to make you obey its passions. **13** Do not present your members to sin as instruments for unrighteousness, but present yourselves to God as those who have been brought from death to life, and your members to God as instruments for righteousness. **14** For sin will have no

cross-ref

O you who love the Lord, hate evil! He preserves the lives of his saints; he delivers them from the hand of the wicked (Psalm 97:10).

---

1. Greek *man*.
2. Greek *has been justified*.

dominion over you, since you are not under law but under grace.

Slaves to Righteousness

15 What then? Are we to sin because we are not under law but under grace? By no means! **16** Do you not know that if you present yourselves to anyone as obedient slaves,[3] you are slaves of the one whom you obey, either of sin, which leads to death, or of obedience, which leads to righteousness? **17** But thanks be to God, that you who were once slaves of sin have become obedient from the heart to the standard of teaching to which you were committed, **18** and, having been set free from sin, have become slaves of righteousness. **19** I am speaking in human terms, because of your natural limitations. For just as you once presented your members as slaves to impurity and to lawlessness leading to more lawlessness, so now present your members as slaves to righteousness leading to sanctification.

20 For when you were slaves of sin, you were free in regard to righteousness. **21** But what fruit were you getting at that time from the things of which you are now ashamed? For the end of those things is death. **22** But now that you have been set free from sin and have become slaves of God, the fruit you get leads to sanctification and its end, eternal life. **23** For the wages of sin is death, but the free gift of God is eternal life in Christ Jesus our Lord.

> **Did you know that** slavery under Mosaic law was not the "harsh slavery" many think of today? It was more like a bankruptcy law — where those lost to debt could sell themselves into slavery/servitude for seven years to cover their debts.

---

3. Greek *bondservants*. Twice in this verse and verse 19; also once in verses 17, 20.

Released from the Law

7 Or do you not know, brothers[1] — for I am speaking to those who know the law — that the law is binding on a person only as long as he lives? [2] For a married woman is bound by law to her husband while he lives, but if her husband dies she is released from the law of marriage.[2] [3] Accordingly, she will be called an adulteress if she lives with another man while her husband is alive. But if her husband dies, she is free from that law, and if she marries another man she is not an adulteress. [4] Likewise, my brothers, you also have died to the law through the body of Christ, so that you may belong to another, to him who has been raised from the dead, in order that we may bear fruit for God. [5] For while we were living in the flesh, our sinful passions, aroused by the law, were at work in our members to bear fruit for death. [6] But now we are released from the law, having died to that which held us captive, so that we serve in the new way of the Spirit and not in the old way of the written code.[3]

> **Did you know the law cannot save you? What the law does is reveal what sin is. It is Christ who saves.**

The Law and Sin

[7] What then shall we say? That the law is sin? By no means! Yet if it had not been for the law, I would not have known sin. For I would not have known what it is to covet if the law had not said, "You shall not covet." [8] But sin, seizing an opportunity through the commandment, produced in me all kinds of covetousness. For apart from the law, sin lies dead. [9] I was once alive apart

---

1. Or brothers and sisters; also verse 4.
2. Greek law concerning the husband.
3. Greek of the letter.

from the law, but when the commandment came, sin came alive and I died. **10** The very commandment that promised life proved to be death to me. **11** For sin, seizing an opportunity through the commandment, deceived me and through it killed me. **12** So the law is holy, and the commandment is holy and righteous and good.

13 Did that which is good, then, bring death to me? By no means! It was sin, producing death in me through what is good, in order that sin might be shown to be sin, and through the commandment might become sinful beyond measure. **14** For we know that the law is spiritual, but I am of the flesh, sold under sin. **15** For I do not understand my own actions. For I do not do what I want, but I do the very thing I hate. **16** Now if I do what I do not want, I agree with the law, that it is good. **17** So now it is no longer I who do it, but sin that dwells within me. **18** For I know that nothing good dwells in me, that is, in my flesh. For I have the desire to do what is right, but not the ability to carry it out. **19** For I do not do the good I want, but the evil I do not want is what I keep on doing. **20** Now if I do what I do not want, it is no longer I who do it, but sin that dwells within me.

21 So I find it to be a law that when I want to do right, evil lies close at hand. **22** For I delight in the law of God, in my inner being, **23** but I see in my members another law waging war against the law of my mind and making me captive to the law of sin that dwells in my members. **24** Wretched man that I am! Who will deliver me from this body of death? **25** Thanks be to God through Jesus Christ our Lord! So then, I myself serve the law of God with my mind, but with my flesh I serve the law of sin.

> **FACT**
>
> Just because one becomes a Christian doesn't mean they don't sin. It does mean they are forgiven — but this is no license to sin.

Life in the Spirit

8 There is therefore now no condemnation for those who are in Christ Jesus.[1] **2** For the law of the Spirit of life has set you[2] free in Christ Jesus from the law of sin and death. **3** For God has done what the law, weakened by the flesh, could not do. By sending his own Son in the likeness of sinful flesh and for sin,[3] he condemned sin in the flesh, **4** in order that the righteous requirement of the law might be fulfilled in us, who walk not according to the flesh but according to the Spirit. **5** For those who live according to the flesh set their minds on the things of the flesh, but those who live according to the Spirit set their minds on the things of the Spirit. **6** For to set the mind on the flesh is death, but to set the mind on the Spirit is life and peace. **7** For the mind that is set on the flesh is hostile to God, for it does not submit to God's law; indeed, it cannot. **8** Those who are in the flesh cannot please God. **9** You, however, are not in the flesh but in the Spirit, if in fact the Spirit of God dwells in you. Anyone who does not have the Spirit of Christ does not belong to him. **10** But if Christ is in you, although the body is dead because of sin, the Spirit is life because of righteousness. **11** If the Spirit of him who raised Jesus[4] from the dead dwells in you, he who raised Christ Jesus from the dead will also give life to your mortal bodies through his Spirit who dwells in you.

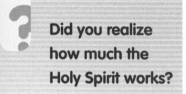

Did you realize how much the Holy Spirit works?

Heirs with Christ

12 So then, brothers,[5] we are debtors, not to the flesh, to live according to the flesh. **13** For if you live according to the

---

1. Some manuscripts add *who walk not according to the flesh (but according to the Spirit)*.
2. Some manuscripts *me*.
3. Or *and as a sin offering*.
4 Some manuscripts lack *Jesus*.
5. Or *brothers and sisters*; also verse 29.

flesh you will die, but if by the Spirit you put to death the deeds of the body, you will live. **14** For all who are led by the Spirit of God are sons of God. **15** For you did not receive the spirit of slavery to fall back into fear, but you have received the Spirit of adoption as sons, by whom we cry, "Abba! Father!" **16** The Spirit himself bears witness with our spirit that we are children of God, **17** and if children, then heirs — heirs of God and fellow heirs with Christ, provided we suffer with him in order that we may also be glorified with him.

Future Glory

18 For I consider that the sufferings of this present time are not worth comparing with the glory that is to be revealed to us. **19** For the creation waits with eager longing for the revealing of the sons of God. **20** For the creation was subjected to futility, not willingly, but because of him who subjected it, in hope **21** that the creation itself will be set free from its bondage to corruption and obtain the freedom of the glory of the children of God. **22** For we know that the whole creation has been groaning together in the pains of childbirth until now. **23** And not only the creation, but we ourselves, who have the firstfruits of the Spirit, groan inwardly as we wait eagerly for adoption as sons, the redemption of our bodies. **24** For in this hope we were saved. Now hope that is seen is not hope. For who hopes for what he sees? **25** But if we hope for what we do not see, we wait for it with patience.

Some ask why God doesn't simply destory all evil immediately. The reason is due to the sons of God (Christians) being revealed throughout the ages. This is but a blink compared to eternity. See Jesus' parable on this topic: Matthew 13:24–43.

26 Likewise the Spirit helps us in our weakness. For we do not know what to pray for as we ought, but the Spirit himself intercedes for us with groanings too deep for words. **27** And he who searches hearts knows what is the mind of the Spirit, because⁶ the Spirit intercedes for the saints according

6. Or that.

to the will of God. **28** And we know that for those who love God all things work together for good,[7] for those who are called according to his purpose. **29** For those whom he foreknew he also predestined to be conformed to the image of his Son, in order that he might be the firstborn among many brothers. **30** And those whom he predestined he also called, and those whom he called he also justified, and those whom he justified he also glorified.

God's Everlasting Love

Did you know God knows the future? God is not bound by time, He created it, which is why God is 100 percent accurate in prophecy (Isaiah 46:10).

31 What then shall we say to these things? If God is for us, who can be[8] against us? **32** He who did not spare his own Son but gave him up for us all, how will he not also with him graciously give us all things? **33** Who shall bring any charge against God's elect? It is God who justifies. **34** Who is to condemn? Christ Jesus is the one who died — more than that, who was raised — who is at the right hand of God, who indeed is interceding for us.[9] **35** Who shall separate us from the love of Christ? Shall tribulation, or distress, or persecution, or famine, or nakedness, or danger, or sword? **36** As it is written,

"For your sake we are being killed all the day long;
we are regarded as sheep to be slaughtered."

37 No, in all these things we are more than conquerors through him who loved us. **38** For I am sure that neither death nor life, nor angels nor rulers, nor things present nor things to come, nor powers, **39** nor height nor depth, nor anything else in all creation, will be able to separate us from the love of God in Christ Jesus our Lord.

7. Some manuscripts *God works all things together for good*, or *God works in all things for the good.*
8. Or *who is.*
9. Or *Is it Christ Jesus who died . . . for us?*

Who Created God?

Some people ask, "Where did God come from?" But this is an illogical question — like asking, "On what page of Shakespeare's book *Hamlet* do you find Shakespeare?" Shakespeare is not confined to his creation (i.e., book) in the same way God is not bound to His creation. When people ask, "Where did God come from?" or "Who created God?" they assume time is absolute and God showed up on the scene at some point, because "come" and "created" are action verbs, which means time is assumed to be in existence.

Since God is uncreated, being the Creator, He is Lord over time and not bound to His creation. So they are illogical questions that try to demote God to being some sort of lesser entity. But that is simply not the God of the Bible.

God's Sovereign Choice

9 I am speaking the truth in Christ — I am not lying; my conscience bears me witness in the Holy Spirit — 2 that I have great sorrow and unceasing anguish in my heart. 3 For I could wish that I myself were accursed and cut off from Christ for the sake of my brothers,[1] my kinsmen according to the flesh. 4 They are Israelites, and to them belong the adoption, the glory, the covenants, the giving of the law, the worship, and the promises. 5 To them belong the patriarchs, and from their race, according to the flesh, is the Christ, who is God over all, blessed forever. Amen. 6 But it is not as though the word of God has failed. For not all who are descended from Israel belong to Israel, 7 and not all are children of Abraham because they are his offspring, but "Through Isaac shall your offspring be named." 8 This means that it is not the children of the flesh who are the children of God, but the children of the promise are counted as offspring. 9 For this is what the promise said: "About this time next year I will return, and Sarah shall have a son." 10 And not only so, but also when Rebekah had conceived children by one man, our forefather Isaac, 11 though they were not yet born and had done nothing either good or bad — in order that God's purpose of election might continue, not because of works but because of him who calls — 12 she was told, "The older will serve the younger." 13 As it is written, "Jacob I loved, but Esau I hated."

> **?** Did you know that when Paul says "race" here he is talking about a people group, not evolutionary higher and lower "races" — a division of people akin to Irish, Chinese, Egyptian, etc.

1. Or brothers and sisters.

14 What shall we say then? Is there injustice on God's part? By no means! **15** For he says to Moses, "I will have mercy on whom I have mercy, and I will have compassion on whom I have compassion." **16** So then it depends not on human will or exertion,[2] but on God, who has mercy. **17** For the Scripture says to Pharaoh, "For this very purpose I have raised you up, that I might show my power in you, and that my name might be proclaimed in all the earth." **18** So then he has mercy on whomever he wills, and he hardens whomever he wills.

19 You will say to me then, "Why does he still find fault? For who can resist his will?" **20** But who are you, O man, to answer back to God? Will what is molded say to its molder, "Why have you made me like this?" **21** Has the potter no right over the clay, to make out of the same lump one vessel for honorable use and another for dishonorable use? **22** What if God, desiring to show his wrath and to make known his power, has endured with much patience vessels of wrath prepared for destruction, **23** in order to make known the riches of his glory for vessels of mercy, which he has prepared beforehand for glory — **24** even us whom he has called, not from the Jews only but also from the Gentiles? **25** As indeed he says in Hosea,

> "Those who were not my people I will call 'my people,' and her who was not beloved I will call 'beloved.'"

cross-ref

You turn things upside down! Shall the potter be regarded as the clay, that the thing made should say of its maker, "He did not make me"; or the thing formed say of him who formed it, "He has no understanding"? (Isaiah 29:16).

---

2. Greek *not of him who wills or runs.*

26 "And in the very place where it was said to
them, 'You are not my people,'
there they will be called 'sons of the living
God.'"

27 And Isaiah cries out concerning Israel: "Though
the number of the sons of Israel[3] be as the sand of the
sea, only a remnant of them will be saved, 28 for the
Lord will carry out his sentence upon the
earth fully and without delay." 29 And as Isaiah
predicted,

> **FACT**
>
> The stumbling block many Jews had was that they thought that by doing works they could earn faith. But it is the other was around. By having faith, then we do work for the Lord, out of love, of course.

"If the Lord of hosts had not left us offspring, we would have been like Sodom
and become like Gomorrah."

Israel's Unbelief

30 What shall we say, then? That Gentiles who did
not pursue righteousness have attained it, that is, a
righteousness that is by faith; 31 but that Israel who pur-
sued a law that would lead to righteousness[4] did not
succeed in reaching that law. 32 Why? Because they did
not pursue it by faith, but as if it were based on works.
They have stumbled over the stumbling stone, 33 as it is
written,

> "Behold, I am laying in Zion a stone
> of stumbling, and a rock of offense;
> and whoever believes in him will not
> be put to shame."

---

3. Or *children of Israel.*
4. Greek *a law of righteousness.*

Do you realize what Paul endured for the gospel?

Are they servants of Christ? I am a better one — I am talking like a madman — with far greater labors, far more imprisonments, with countless beatings, and often near death. Five times I received at the hands of the Jews the forty lashes less one. Three times I was beaten with rods. Once I was stoned. Three times I was shipwrecked; a night and a day I was adrift at sea; on frequent journeys, in danger from rivers, danger from robbers, danger from my own people, danger from Gentiles, danger in the city, danger in the wilderness, danger at sea, danger from false brothers; in toil and hardship, through many a sleepless night, in hunger and thirst, often without food, in cold and exposure. And, apart from other things, there is the daily pressure on me of my anxiety for all the churches (2 Corinthians 11:23–28).

How does this make you feel?

But be on your guard. For they will deliver you over to councils, and you will be beaten in synagogues, and you will stand before governors and kings for my sake, to bear witness before them (Mark 13:9).

10 Brothers,[1] my heart's desire and prayer to God for them is that they may be saved. 2 For I bear them witness that they have a zeal for God, but not according to knowledge. 3 For, being ignorant of the righteousness of God, and seeking to establish their own, they did not submit to God's righteousness. 4 For Christ is the end of the law for righteousness to everyone who believes.[2]

cross-ref

In him you also, when you heard the word of truth, the gospel of your salvation, and believed in him, were sealed with the promised Holy Spirit (Ephesians 1:13).

The Message of Salvation to All

5 For Moses writes about the righteousness that is based on the law, that the person who does the commandments shall live by them. 6 But the righteousness based on faith says, "Do not say in your heart, 'Who will ascend into heaven?' " (that is, to bring Christ down) 7 "or 'Who will descend into the abyss?' " (that is, to bring Christ up from the dead). 8 But what does it say? "The word is near you, in your mouth and in your heart" (that is, the word of faith that we proclaim); 9 because, if you confess with your mouth that Jesus is Lord and believe in your heart that God raised him from the dead, you will be saved. 10 For with the heart one believes and is justified, and with the mouth one confesses and is saved. 11 For the Scripture says, "Everyone who believes in him will not be put to shame." 12 For there is no distinction between Jew and Greek; for the same Lord is Lord of all, bestowing his riches on all who call on him. 13 For "everyone who calls on the name of the Lord will be saved."

---

1. Or Brothers and sisters.
2. Or end of the law, that everyone who believes may be justified.

14 How then will they call on him in whom they have not believed? And how are they to believe in him of whom they have never heard?[3] And how are they to hear without someone preaching? **15** And how are they to preach unless they are sent? As it is written, "How beautiful are the feet of those who preach the good news!" **16** But they have not all obeyed the gospel. For Isaiah says, "Lord, who has believed what he has heard from us?" **17** So faith comes from hearing, and hearing through the word of Christ.

18 But I ask, have they not heard? Indeed they have, for

"Their voice has gone out to all the earth,
and their words to the ends of the world."

19 But I ask, did Israel not understand? First Moses says,

"I will make you jealous of those who are not
a nation;
with a foolish nation I will make
you angry."

20 Then Isaiah is so bold as to say,

"I have been found by those who
did not seek me;
I have shown myself to those who
did not ask for me."

21 But of Israel he says, "All day long I have held out my hands to a disobedient and contrary people."

Do you realize how broken-hearted Paul was that his fellow Jews refused Christ?

---

3. Or *him whom they have never heard.*

The Remnant of Israel

11 I ask, then, has God rejected his people? By no means! For I myself am an Israelite, a descendant of Abraham,[1] a member of the tribe of Benjamin. 2 God has not rejected his people whom he foreknew. Do you not know what the Scripture says of Elijah, how he appeals to God against Israel? 3 "Lord, they have killed your prophets, they have demolished your altars, and I alone am left, and they seek my life." 4 But what is God's reply to him? "I have kept for myself seven thousand men who have not bowed the knee to Baal." 5 So too at the present time there is a remnant, chosen by grace. 6 But if it is by grace, it is no longer on the basis of works; otherwise grace would no longer be grace. 7 What then? Israel failed to obtain what it was seeking. The elect obtained it, but the rest were hardened, 8 as it is written,

> "God gave them a spirit of stupor,
> eyes that would not see
> and ears that would not hear,
> down to this very day."

9 And David says,

> "Let their table become a snare and a trap,
> a stumbling block and a retribution for them;
> 10 let their eyes be darkened so that they
> cannot see,
> and bend their backs forever."

With the Flood and with the Israelites in the desert there was a remnant. In Elijah's day there was a remnant. And in Paul's day there was a remnant of Jews, including Paul, who became Christians (Romans 1:16).

---

1. Or *one of the offspring of Abraham.*

Gentiles Grafted In

11 So I ask, did they stumble in order that they might fall? By no means! Rather through their trespass salvation has come to the Gentiles, so as to make Israel jealous. **12** Now if their trespass means riches for the world, and if their failure means riches for the Gentiles, how much more will their full inclusion[2] mean!

13 Now I am speaking to you Gentiles. Inasmuch then as I am an apostle to the Gentiles, I magnify my ministry **14** in order somehow to make my fellow Jews jealous, and thus save some of them. **15** For if their rejection means the reconciliation of the world, what will their acceptance mean but life from the dead? **16** If the dough offered as firstfruits is holy, so is the whole lump, and if the root is holy, so are the branches.

17 But if some of the branches were broken off, and you, although a wild olive shoot, were grafted in among the others and now share in the nourishing root[3] of the olive tree, **18** do not be arrogant toward the branches. If you are, remember it is not you who support the root, but the root that supports you. **19** Then you will say, "Branches were broken off so that I might be grafted in." **20** That is true. They were broken off because of their unbelief, but you stand fast through faith. So do not become proud, but fear. **21** For if God did not spare the natural branches, neither will he spare you. **22** Note then the kindness and the severity of God: severity toward

> **FACT**
>
> Gentiles were typically those people who were not Jews (i.e., not Israelites).

---

2. Greek *their fullness.*
3. Greek *root of richness*; some manuscripts *richness.*

those who have fallen, but God's kindness to you, provided you continue in his kindness. Otherwise you too will be cut off. **23** And even they, if they do not continue in their unbelief, will be grafted in, for God has the power to graft them in again. **24** For if you were cut from what is by nature a wild olive tree, and grafted, contrary to nature, into a cultivated olive tree, how much more will these, the natural branches, be grafted back into their own olive tree.

The Mystery of Israel's Salvation

25 Lest you be wise in your own sight, I do not want you to be unaware of this mystery, brothers:[4] a partial hardening has come upon Israel, until the fullness of the Gentiles has come in. **26** And in this way all Israel will be saved, as it is written,

"The Deliverer will come from Zion,
he will banish ungodliness from Jacob";
27 "and this will be my covenant with them
when I take away their sins."

28 As regards the gospel, they are enemies for your sake. But as regards election, they are beloved for the sake of their forefathers. **29** For the gifts and the calling of God are irrevocable. **30** For just as you were at one time disobedient to God but now have received mercy because of their disobedience, **31** so they too have now been disobedient in order that by the mercy shown to

cross-ref

But the Scripture imprisoned everything under sin, so that the promise by faith in Jesus Christ might be given to those who believe (Galatians 3:22).

---

4. Or *brothers and sisters.*

you they also may now[5] receive mercy. **32** For God has consigned all to disobedience, that he may have mercy on all.

33 Oh, the depth of the riches and wisdom and knowledge of God! How unsearchable are his judgments and how inscrutable his ways!

> **34** "For who has known the mind of the Lord,
> or who has been his counselor?"

> **35** "Or who has given a gift to him
> that he might be repaid?"

36 For from him and through him and to him are all things. To him be glory forever. Amen.

For then he would have had to suffer repeatedly since the foundation of the world. But as it is, he has appeared once for all at the end of the ages to put away sin by the sacrifice of himself. And just as it is appointed for man to die once, and after that comes judgment, so Christ, having been offered once to bear the sins of many, will appear a second time, not to deal with sin but to save those who are eagerly waiting for him (Hebrews 9:26–28).

---

5. Some manuscripts omit *now*.

A Living Sacrifice

12 I appeal to you therefore, brothers,[1] by the mercies of God, to present your bodies as a living sacrifice, holy and acceptable to God, which is your spiritual worship.[2] **2** Do not be conformed to this world,[3] but be transformed by the renewal of your mind, that by testing you may discern what is the will of God, what is good and acceptable and perfect.[4]

Did you know that our bodies are important because the body is now the temple of the Holy Spirit that lives in us? (1 Corinthians 3:16 and 6:19).

Gifts of Grace

3 For by the grace given to me I say to everyone among you not to think of himself more highly than he ought to think, but to think with sober judgment, each according to the measure of faith that God has assigned. **4** For as in one body we have many members,[5] and the members do not all have the same function, **5** so we, though many, are one body in Christ, and individually members one of another. **6** Having gifts that differ according to the grace given to us, let us use them: if prophecy, in proportion to our faith; **7** if service, in our serving; the one who teaches, in his teaching; **8** the one who exhorts, in his exhortation; the one who contributes, in generosity; the one who leads,[6] with zeal; the one who does acts of mercy, with cheerfulness.

---

1. Or brothers and sisters.
2. Or your rational service.
3. Greek age.
4. Or what is the good and acceptable and perfect will of God.
5. Greek parts; also verse 5.
6. Or gives aid.

Marks of the True Christian

9 Let love be genuine. Abhor what is evil; hold fast to what is good. **10** Love one another with brotherly affection. Outdo one another in showing honor. **11** Do not be slothful in zeal, be fervent in spirit,[7] serve the Lord. **12** Rejoice in hope, be patient in tribulation, be constant in prayer. **13** Contribute to the needs of the saints and seek to show hospitality.

14 Bless those who persecute you; bless and do not curse them. **15** Rejoice with those who rejoice, weep with those who weep. **16** Live in harmony with one another. Do not be haughty, but associate with the lowly.[8] Never be wise in your own sight. **17** Repay no one evil for evil, but give thought to do what is honorable in the sight of all. **18** If possible, so far as it depends on you, live peaceably with all. **19** Beloved, never avenge yourselves, but leave it[9] to the wrath of God, for it is written, "Vengeance is mine, I will repay, says the Lord." **20** To the contrary, "if your enemy is hungry, feed him; if he is thirsty, give him something to drink; for by so doing you will heap burning coals on his head." **21** Do not be overcome by evil, but overcome evil with good.

> **FACT**
>
> Christians are to leave vengeance to God. God is the perfect judge and will do what is best.

---

7. Or *fervent in the Spirit.*
8. Or *give yourselves to humble tasks.*
9. Greek *give place.*

Submission to the Authorities

13 Let every person be subject to the governing authorities. For there is no authority except from God, and those that exist have been instituted by God. **2** Therefore whoever resists the authorities resists what God has appointed, and those who resist will incur judgment. **3** For rulers are not a terror to good conduct, but to bad. Would you have no fear of the one who is in authority? Then do what is good, and you will receive his approval, **4** for he is God's servant for your good. But if you do wrong, be afraid, for he does not bear the sword in vain. For he is the servant of God, an avenger who carries out God's wrath on the wrongdoer. **5** Therefore one must be in subjection, not only to avoid God's wrath but also for the sake of conscience. **6** For because of this you also pay taxes, for the authorities are ministers of God, attending to this very thing. **7** Pay to all what is owed to them: taxes to whom taxes are owed, revenue to whom revenue is owed, respect to whom respect is owed, honor to whom honor is owed.

> **cross-ref**
>
> **Regarding love, Paul is affirming what Jesus taught in John 13:34–35.**

Fulfilling the Law Through Love

8 Owe no one anything, except to love each other, for the one who loves another has fulfilled the law. **9** For the commandments, "You shall not commit adultery, You shall not murder, You shall not steal, You shall not covet," and any other commandment, are summed up in this word: "You shall love your neighbor as yourself." **10** Love does no wrong to a neighbor; therefore love is the fulfilling of the law.

¹¹ Besides this you know the time, that the hour has come for you to wake from sleep. For salvation is nearer to us now than when we first believed. ¹² The night is far gone; the day is at hand. So then let us cast off the works of darkness and put on the armor of light. ¹³ Let us walk properly as in the daytime, not in orgies and drunkenness, not in sexual immorality and sensuality, not in quarreling and jealousy. ¹⁴ But put on the Lord Jesus Christ, and make no provision for the flesh, to gratify its desires.

As the Law is summed up in "Love your neighbor as yourself," one should refrain from sin.

FACT

Do Not Pass Judgment on One Another

14 As for the one who is weak in faith, welcome him, but not to quarrel over opinions. ² One person believes he may eat anything, while the weak person eats only vegetables. ³ Let not the one who eats despise the one who abstains, and let not the one who abstains pass judgment on the one who eats, for God has welcomed him. ⁴ Who are you to pass judgment on the servant of another? It is before his own master[1] that he stands or falls. And he will be upheld, for the Lord is able to make him stand. ⁵ One person esteems one day as better than another, while another esteems all days alike. Each one should be fully convinced in his own mind. ⁶ The one who observes the day, observes it in honor of the Lord. The one who eats, eats in honor of the Lord, since he gives thanks to God, while the one who abstains, abstains in honor of the Lord and gives thanks to God. ⁷ For none of us lives to himself, and none of us dies to himself. ⁸ For if we live, we live to the Lord, and if we die, we die to the Lord. So then, whether we live or whether we die, we are the Lord's. ⁹ For to this end Christ died and lived again, that he might be Lord both of the dead and of the living.

¹⁰ Why do you pass judgment on your brother? Or you, why do you despise your brother? For we will all stand before the judgment seat of God; ¹¹ for it is written,

"As I live, says the Lord, every knee shall bow to me,

cross-ref

Notice Paul's advice on how to love one another. There were quarrels over eating clean and unclean meat, and when to worship — Jewish Sabbath or Sunday in honor of the Resurrection (Acts 20:7; 1 Corinithians 16:2).

---

1. Or lord.

and every tongue shall confess[2] to God."
12 So then each of us will give an account of himself to God.

Do Not Cause Another to Stumble

13 Therefore let us not pass judgment on one another any longer, but rather decide never to put a stumbling block or hindrance in the way of a brother. **14** I know and am persuaded in the Lord Jesus that nothing is unclean in itself, but it is unclean for anyone who thinks it unclean. **15** For if your brother is grieved by what you eat, you are no longer walking in love. By what you eat, do not destroy the one for whom Christ died. **16** So do not let what you regard as good be spoken of as evil. **17** For the kingdom of God is not a matter of eating and drinking but of righteousness and peace and joy in the Holy Spirit. **18** Whoever thus serves Christ is acceptable to God and approved by men. **19** So then let us pursue what makes for peace and for mutual upbuilding.

20 Do not, for the sake of food, destroy the work of God. Everything is indeed clean, but it is wrong for anyone to make another stumble by what he eats. **21** It is good not to eat meat or drink wine or do anything that causes your brother to stumble.[3] **22** The faith that you have, keep between yourself and God. Blessed is the one who has no reason to pass judgment on himself for what he approves. **23** But whoever has doubts is condemned if he eats, because the eating is not from faith. For whatever does not proceed from faith is sin.[4]

FACT

Paul is continuing to point out that one should not intentionally cause a brother to stumble, but rather take the time to explain to them why something is not evil.

---

2. Or *shall give praise.*
3. Some manuscripts add *or be hindered or be weakened.*
4. Some manuscripts insert here 16:25–27.

The Example of Christ

15 We who are strong have an obligation to bear with the failings of the weak, and not to please ourselves. 2 Let each of us please his neighbor for his good, to build him up. 3 For Christ did not please himself, but as it is written, "The reproaches of those who reproached you fell on me." 4 For whatever was written in former days was written for our instruction, that through endurance and through the encouragement of the Scriptures we might have hope. 5 May the God of endurance and encouragement grant you to live in such harmony with one another, in accord with Christ Jesus, 6 that together you may with one voice glorify the God and Father of our Lord Jesus Christ. 7 Therefore welcome one another as Christ has welcomed you, for the glory of God.

> **cross-ref**
> Therefore let it be known to you that this salvation of God has been sent to the Gentiles; they will listen (Acts 28:28).

Christ the Hope of Jews and Gentiles

8 For I tell you that Christ became a servant to the circumcised to show God's truthfulness, in order to confirm the promises given to the patriarchs, 9 and in order that the Gentiles might glorify God for his mercy. As it is written,

> "Therefore I will praise you among the Gentiles,
> and sing to your name."

10 And again it is said,

> "Rejoice, O Gentiles, with his people."

11 And again,

> "Praise the Lord, all you Gentiles,
> and let all the peoples extol him."

12 And again Isaiah says,

> "The root of Jesse will come,
> even he who arises to rule the Gentiles;
> in him will the Gentiles hope."

13 May the God of hope fill you with all joy and peace in believing, so that by the power of the Holy Spirit you may abound in hope.

Paul the Minister to the Gentiles

14 I myself am satisfied about you, my brothers,[1] that you yourselves are full of goodness, filled with all knowledge and able to instruct one another. **15** But on some points I have written to you very boldly by way of reminder, because of the grace given me by God **16** to be a minister of Christ Jesus to the Gentiles in the priestly service of the gospel of God, so that the offering of the Gentiles may be acceptable, sanctified by the Holy Spirit. **17** In Christ Jesus, then, I have reason to be proud of my work for God. **18** For I will not venture to speak of anything except what Christ has accomplished through me to bring the Gentiles to obedience—by word and deed, **19** by the power of signs and wonders, by the power of the Spirit of God — so that from Jerusalem and all the way around to Illyricum I have fulfilled the ministry of the gospel of Christ; **20** and thus I make it my ambition to preach the

FACT

Jesus is the root of Jesse. Jesus' lineage goes back to David and David's father was Jesse.

---

1. Or *brothers and sisters*; also verse 30.

gospel, not where Christ has already been named, lest I build on someone else's foundation, **21** but as it is written,

"Those who have never been told of him will see,
and those who have never heard will understand."

Paul's Plan to Visit Rome

FACT

Paul had plans to go to Spain. Many have debated if Paul went to Spain and came back to Rome, but the Bible doesn't say. Church fathers say Paul died in Rome.

22 This is the reason why I have so often been hindered from coming to you. **23** But now, since I no longer have any room for work in these regions, and since I have longed for many years to come to you, **24** I hope to see you in passing as I go to Spain, and to be helped on my journey there by you, once I have enjoyed your company for a while. **25** At present, however, I am going to Jerusalem bringing aid to the saints. **26** For Macedonia and Achaia have been pleased to make some contribution for the poor among the saints at Jerusalem. **27** For they were pleased to do it, and indeed they owe it to them. For if the Gentiles have come to share in their spiritual blessings, they ought also to be of service to them in material blessings. **28** When therefore I have completed this and have delivered to them what has been collected,[2] I will leave for Spain by way of you. **29** I know that when I come to you I will come in the fullness of the blessing[3] of Christ.

30 I appeal to you, brothers, by our Lord Jesus Christ and by the love of the Spirit, to strive together with me in your prayers to God on my behalf, **31** that I

---

2. Greek *sealed to them this fruit.*
3. Some manuscripts insert *of the gospel.*

may be delivered from the unbelievers in Judea, and that my service for Jerusalem may be acceptable to the saints, ³² so that by God's will I may come to you with joy and be refreshed in your company. ³³ May the God of peace be with you all. Amen.

Paul's trip to Rome was classed as his fourth missionary journey.

FACT

Personal Greetings

16 I commend to you our sister Phoebe, a servant[1] of the church at Cenchreae, **2** that you may welcome her in the Lord in a way worthy of the saints, and help her in whatever she may need from you, for she has been a patron of many and of myself as well. **3** Greet Prisca and Aquila, my fellow workers in Christ Jesus, **4** who risked their necks for my life, to whom not only I give thanks but all the churches of the Gentiles give thanks as well. **5** Greet also the church in their house. Greet my beloved Epaenetus, who was the first convert[2] to Christ in Asia. **6** Greet Mary, who has worked hard for you. **7** Greet Andronicus and Junia,[3] my kinsmen and my fellow prisoners. They are well known to the apostles,[4] and they were in Christ before me. **8** Greet Ampliatus, my beloved in the Lord. **9** Greet Urbanus, our fellow worker in Christ, and my beloved Stachys. **10** Greet Apelles, who is approved in Christ. Greet those who belong to the family of Aristobulus. **11** Greet my kinsman Herodion. Greet those in the Lord who belong to the family of Narcissus. **12** Greet those workers in the Lord, Tryphaena and Tryphosa. Greet the beloved Persis, who has worked hard in the Lord. **13** Greet Rufus, chosen in the Lord; also his mother, who has been a mother to me as well. **14** Greet Asyncritus, Phlegon, Hermes, Patrobas, Hermas, and the brothers[5] who are with them. **15** Greet Philologus, Julia, Nereus and his sister, and Olympas, and all the saints

FACT

Christians went to Rome because it was the center of the world at that time. It was an ideal place to witness to people of virtually every tongue and tribe.

---

1. Or *deaconess.*
2. Greek *firstfruit.*
3. Or *Junias.*
4. Or *messengers.*
5. Or *brothers and sisters;* also verse 17.

who are with them. **16** Greet one another with a holy kiss. All the churches of Christ greet you.

Final Instructions and Greetings

17 I appeal to you, brothers, to watch out for those who cause divisions and create obstacles contrary to the doctrine that you have been taught; avoid them. **18** For such persons do not serve our Lord Christ, but their own appetites,[6] and by smooth talk and flattery they deceive the hearts of the naive. **19** For your obedience is known to all, so that I rejoice over you, but I want you to be wise as to what is good and innocent as to what is evil. **20** The God of peace will soon crush Satan under your feet. The grace of our Lord Jesus Christ be with you.

21 Timothy, my fellow worker, greets you; so do Lucius and Jason and Sosipater, my kinsmen.

22 I Tertius, who wrote this letter, greet you in the Lord.

23 Gaius, who is host to me and to the whole church, greets you. Erastus, the city treasurer, and our brother Quartus, greet you.[7]

Doxology

25 Now to him who is able to strengthen you according to my gospel and the preaching of Jesus Christ, according to the revelation of the mystery that was kept secret for long ages **26** but has now been disclosed and through the prophetic writings has been made known to all nations, according to the command of the eternal God, to bring about the obedience of faith — **27** to the only wise God be glory forevermore through Jesus Christ! Amen.

FACT

Those who cause divisions are those who are going against what the Bible teaches (doctrines).

6. Greek *their own belly*.

7. Some manuscripts insert verse 24: *The grace of our Lord Jesus Christ be with you all. Amen.*

From Paul's Letter to the Romans to John's Vision of the Apocalypse(Revelation)

As the Apostolic period was coming to a close, the books of the New Testament, primarily letters and the Gospels, were completed and being copied in great numbers so Christians could read them. Most of the Apostles had been killed for their faith (whether by sword, arrows, crucifixion, etc.). For example, church fathers reveal that Peter was crucified upside-down, and Paul was beheaded.[1]

But John, unlike most of the other Apostles, lived and died a natural death. The last book of the Bible is a vision John had in the Spirit while banished for his faith to an island called Patmos in the Aegean Sea (Revelation 1:9).[2] Revelation is a prophetic book that discusses things John saw, things that were, and things that were to come.

The Church as a whole was struggling and under severe persecution from the Roman Empire at the time. John wrote this book to several churches in Asia Minor (modern-day Turkey) about events that were to begin shortly (Revelation 1:1–4)[3] as well as a prelude to what heaven will be like (Revelation 21 and 22). It gives Christians an idea of what to look forward to. The last two chapters of the Book of Revelation make a great finish to Scriptures as a whole.

---

1   For more on this, see Josh McDowell's *More than a Carpenter* (Carol Stream, IL: Tyndale House Publishers, 1977/2005).

2   Revelation 1:9: I, John, your brother and partner in the tribulation and the kingdom and the patient endurance that are in Jesus, was on the island called Patmos on account of the word of God and the testimony of Jesus.

3   Revelation 1:1–3: The revelation of Jesus Christ, which God gave him to show to his servants the things that must soon take place. He made it known by sending his angel to his servant John, who bore witness to the word of God and to the testimony of Jesus Christ, even to all that he saw. Blessed is the one who reads aloud the words of this prophecy, and blessed are those who hear, and who keep what is written in it, for the time is near.

The Revelation To John

The New Heaven and the New Earth

21 Then I saw a new heaven and a new earth, for the first heaven and the first earth had passed away, and the sea was no more. **2** And I saw the holy city, new Jerusalem, coming down out of heaven from God, prepared as a bride adorned for her husband. **3** And I heard a loud voice from the throne saying, "Behold, the dwelling place[1] of God is with man. He will dwell with them, and they will be his people,[2] and God himself will be with them as their God.[3] **4** He will wipe away every tear from their eyes, and death shall be no more, neither shall there be mourning, nor crying, nor pain anymore, for the former things have passed away." **5** And he who was seated on the throne said, "Behold, I am making all things new." Also he said, "Write this down, for these words are trustworthy and true." **6** And he said to me, "It is done! I am the Alpha and the Omega, the beginning and the end. To the thirsty I will give from the spring of the water of life without payment. **7** The one who conquers will have this heritage, and I will be his God and he will be my son. **8** But as for the cowardly, the faithless, the detestable, as for murderers, the sexually immoral, sorcerers, idolaters, and all liars, their portion will be in the lake that burns with fire and sulfur, which is the second death."

> **cross-ref**
>
> For behold, I create new heavens and a new earth, and the former things shall not be remembered or come into mind (Isaiah 65:17).

---

1. Or *tabernacle*.
2. Some manuscripts *peoples*.
3. Some manuscripts omit *as their God*.

The New Jerusalem

9 Then came one of the seven angels who had the seven bowls full of the seven last plagues and spoke to me, saying, "Come, I will show you the Bride, the wife of the Lamb." **10** And he carried me away in the Spirit to a great, high mountain, and showed me the holy city Jerusalem coming down out of heaven from God, **11** having the glory of God, its radiance like a most rare jewel, like a jasper, clear as crystal. **12** It had a great, high wall, with twelve gates, and at the gates twelve angels, and on the gates the names of the twelve tribes of the sons of Israel were inscribed — **13** on the east three gates, on the north three gates, on the south three gates, and on the west three gates. **14** And the wall of the city had twelve foundations, and on them were the twelve names of the twelve apostles of the Lamb.

15 And the one who spoke with me had a measuring rod of gold to measure the city and its gates and walls. **16** The city lies foursquare, its length the same as its width. And he measured the city with his rod, 12,000 stadia.[4] Its length and width and height are equal. **17** He also measured its wall, 144 cubits[5] by human measurement, which is also an angel's measurement. **18** The wall was built of jasper, while the city was pure gold, like clear glass. **19** The foundations of the wall of the city were adorned with every kind of jewel. The first was jasper, the second sapphire, the third agate, the fourth emerald, **20** the fifth onyx, the sixth carnelian, the seventh chrysolite, the eighth beryl, the ninth topaz, the tenth chrysoprase, the eleventh jacinth, the twelfth amethyst. **21** And the twelve gates were twelve pearls, each of the gates

> **FACT**
>
> Obviously, there is some metaphorical language here and this is expected, being a prophetic book. For example, 12,000 stadia is about 1,400 miles — the space station orbits at 220 miles! The point is, the New Jerusalem is huge!

---

4.   About 1,380 miles; a *stadion* was about 607 feet or 185 meters.
5.   A *cubit* was about 18 inches or 45 centimeters.

made of a single pearl, and the street of the city was pure gold, like transparent glass.

²²And I saw no temple in the city, for its temple is the Lord God the Almighty and the Lamb. ²³And the city has no need of sun or moon to shine on it, for the glory of God gives it light, and its lamp is the Lamb. ²⁴By its light will the nations walk, and the kings of the earth will bring their glory into it, ²⁵and its gates will never be shut by day — and there will be no night there. ²⁶They will bring into it the glory and the honor of the nations. ²⁷But nothing unclean will ever enter it, nor anyone who does what is detestable or false, but only those who are written in the Lamb's book of life.

FACT

No more death or crying or pain — this is something to look forward to.

We needed a new heavens and a new earth because this one has been marred with sin and the Curse back in Genesis 3. Romans 8:20–22 gives the extent of sin — the "whole creation groans." This is why things need to be made new (Revelation 21:5).

But when Christ appeared as a high priest of the good things that have come, then through the greater and more perfect tent (not made with hands, that is, not of this creation) he entered once for all into the holy places, not by means of the blood of goats and calves but by means of his own blood, thus securing an eternal redemption (Hebrews 9:11–12).

The River of Life

22 Then the angel[1] showed me the river of the water of life, bright as crystal, flowing from the throne of God and of the Lamb **2** through the middle of the street of the city; also, on either side of the river, the tree of life[2] with its twelve kinds of fruit, yielding its fruit each month. The leaves of the tree were for the healing of the nations. **3** No longer will there be anything accursed, but the throne of God and of the Lamb will be in it, and his servants[3] will worship him. **4** They will see his face, and his name will be on their foreheads. **5** And night will be no more. They will need no light of lamp or sun, for the Lord God will be their light, and they will reign forever and ever.

cross-ref

Verse 3 points out the curse ("accursed") will be removed. In essence, what happened in the third chapter of the Bible is being reversed in the last two chapters of the Bible.

Jesus Is Coming

6 And he said to me, "These words are trustworthy and true. And the Lord, the God of the spirits of the prophets, has sent his angel to show his servants what must soon take place."

7 "And behold, I am coming soon. Blessed is the one who keeps the words of the prophecy of this book."

8 I, John, am the one who heard and saw these things. And when I heard and saw them, I fell down to worship at the feet of the angel who showed them to me, **9** but he said to me, "You must not do that! I am a fellow servant[4] with you and your brothers the prophets, and with those who keep the words of this book. Worship God."

10 And he said to me, "Do not seal up the words of the prophecy of this book, for the time is near. **11** Let the evildoer

---

1. Greek *he*.
2. Or *the Lamb. In the midst of the street of the city, and on either side of the river, was the tree of life*.
3. Greek *bondservants*; also verse 6.
4. Greek *fellow bondservant*.

still do evil, and the filthy still be filthy, and the righteous still do right, and the holy still be holy."

12"Behold, I am coming soon, bringing my recompense with me, to repay each one for what he has done. **13**I am the Alpha and the Omega, the first and the last, the beginning and the end."

14Blessed are those who wash their robes,[5] so that they may have the right to the tree of life and that they may enter the city by the gates. **15**Outside are the dogs and sorcerers and the sexually immoral and murderers and idolaters, and everyone who loves and practices falsehood.

16"I, Jesus, have sent my angel to testify to you about these things for the churches. I am the root and the descendant of David, the bright morning star."

17The Spirit and the Bride say, "Come." And let the one who hears say, "Come." And let the one who is thirsty come; let the one who desires take the water of life without price.

18I warn everyone who hears the words of the prophecy of this book: if anyone adds to them, God will add to him the plagues described in this book, **19**and if anyone takes away from the words of the book of this prophecy, God will take away his share in the tree of life and in the holy city, which are described in this book.

Is your name written in the Lamb's book of life? In other words, are you saved?

20He who testifies to these things says, "Surely I am coming soon." Amen. Come, Lord Jesus!

21The grace of the Lord Jesus be with all.[6] Amen.

---

5. Some manuscripts *do his commandments.*
6. Some manuscripts *all the saints.*

What Does It Mean to Be Saved?

A re you like me? I get tired of sitting down in the middle of something like a story, show, etc., and wondering what's going on. I think most people feel like this when they hear about Jesus for the first time. In my past, I would hear things like: "Good news! Good news! Here's how to get saved: Believe in Jesus!"

I was thinking, *Saved from what? Jesus who?* Obviously, there was something missing in the approach that these well-meaning Christians used with me, and it is important, then, to learn to be better witnesses.

Perfect Creation . . . Then the Bad News

First of all, it's tough to understand the good news of being saved if you don't understand the bad news. So let's go back to the beginning. In the beginning, God created everything:

Genesis 1:1
In the beginning, God created the heavens and the earth. (See also John 1:1–3.)

When God created everything, He said it was "very good." This meant that everything was perfect. The whole creation was perfect. In fact, God says that all His works are perfect, and we would expect that from a perfect God. Man lived in the perfectly created earth (i.e., a paradise) with a perfect relationship with God.

Genesis 1:31
And God saw everything that he had made, and behold, it was very good. And there was evening and there was morning, the sixth day. (See also Deuteronomy 32:4.)

Since the original creation was perfect, there was no death before this (Genesis 1:29–30)[1] God gave people the freedom of contrary choice.[2] The first two people God created were Adam and Eve, who were allowed to freely eat from any tree in the Garden of Eden except the Tree of the Knowledge of Good and Evil. They were to live forever with God. Again, there was no death. However, Eve was tempted by a serpent (being influenced by Satan, who had rebelled against God in the heavenly realm), and then both Adam and Eve also rebelled against God by eating from the Tree of the Knowledge of Good and Evil; thus, they sinned (sin is rebellion against God).[3]

Genesis 2:16–17
And the LORD God commanded the man, saying, "You may surely eat of every tree of the garden, but of the tree of the knowledge of good and evil you shall not eat, for in the day that you eat of it you shall surely die."

Genesis 3:1–6
Now the serpent was more crafty than any other beast of the field that the LORD God had made. He said to the woman, "Did God actually say, 'You shall not eat of any tree in the garden'?" And the woman said to the serpent, "We may eat of the fruit of the trees in the garden, but God said, 'You shall not eat of the fruit of the tree that is in the midst of the garden, neither shall you touch it, lest you die.'" But the serpent said to the woman, "You will not surely die. For God knows that when you eat of it your eyes will be opened, and you will be like God, knowing good and evil." So when the woman saw that the tree was good for food, and that it was a delight to the

1. Ken Ham, "Two Histories of Death," *Creation* 24(1):18–20, December, 2001, online here: http://www.answersingenesis.org/creation/v24/i1/history.asp.
2. Whether this is still the case has been up for debate for centuries and is not for discussion in this short article.
3. Bodie Hodge, "Feedback: Who Sinned First?" March 14, 2008, online here: http://www.answersingenesis.org/articles/2008/03/14/feedback-first-sin.

eyes, and that the tree was to be desired to make one wise, she took of its fruit and ate, and she also gave some to her husband who was with her, and he ate.

The result of Adam's sin (rebellion against a holy Creator) was God's judgment through many curses. God cursed the ground, which mankind had dominion over (Genesis 1:28), to bring forth thorns and thistles. He sentenced man and woman to die, fulfilling what was spoken in Genesis 2:17. He also cursed the animals, especially the serpent.

From this act of rebellion, we (i.e., humans, descendants of Adam) inherited "original sin." This, in a layman's sense, means that we are sentenced to die and are prone to sin because we were in Adam when he sinned (see also Hebrews 7:9–11 and 1 Corinthians 15:22). In essence, these curses are like God removing some of His sustaining power, so the creation is no longer upheld in a perfect state but is in bondage to sin and death (Romans 8:21). Hence, we now suffer with things like cancer, sickness, suffering, and finally, death.

Genesis 3:14–19
The LORD God said to the serpent, "Because you have done this, cursed are you above all livestock and above all beasts of the field; on your belly you shall go, and dust you shall eat all the days of your life. I will put enmity between you and the woman, and between your offspring and her offspring; he shall bruise your head, and you shall bruise his heel." To the woman he said, "I will surely multiply your pain in childbearing; in pain you shall bring forth children. Your desire shall be for your husband, and he shall rule over you." And to Adam he said, "Because you have listened to the voice of your wife and have eaten of the tree of which I commanded you, 'You shall not eat of it,' cursed is the ground because of you; in pain you shall eat of it all the days of your life; thorns and thistles

it shall bring forth for you; and you shall eat the plants of the field. By the sweat of your face you shall eat bread, till you return to the ground, for out of it you were taken; for you are dust, and to dust you shall return."

Romans 5:12
Therefore, just as sin came into the world through one man, and death through sin, and so death spread to all men because all sinned.

In spite of our sin, God loved us so much that He had already planned a way for us to return to a perfect relationship with Him. To provide forgiveness and salvation, God gave the first prophecy of many regarding the way back to a restored relationship with Him. Genesis 3:15 says that the *seed* will be that of a woman (see also Isaiah 7:14). This refers to the future event — the virgin birth of Jesus — being the "seed of a woman" and not of a man.

Death and Sacrifice Point Toward a Savior

In the New Testament, Paul confirms what is written in Genesis 2:17 when he says that the wages of sin is death. One sin is enough to cause death!

Romans 6:23
For the wages of sin is death. . . .

Since the wages of sin is death, God, in Genesis 3, shows that a life must be taken to cover the sin of Adam and Eve. Therefore, to make a temporary atonement (cover the sins for a time), God killed these animals on behalf of Adam and Eve, clothing them with the skins.

Genesis 3:21
And the Lord God made for Adam and for his wife garments of skins and clothed them.

The punishment demanded from an infinitely holy God who cannot look upon sin is an infinite punishment. Animals are not infinite, and so they cannot ultimately take away sin but merely cover it. Mankind needed a perfect, infinitely holy sacrifice. Jesus Christ, who is the infinite and holy Son of God, stepped into history to take that punishment on Himself. We ultimately need a perfect sacrifice, and the perfectly obedient life of Christ was God's plan for the ultimate atonement.

But after Adam and Eve sinned, people began making animal sacrifices to cover their sins — an animal life for sin. A few examples follow.

Abel
Genesis 4:4: and Abel also brought of the firstborn of his flock and of their fat portions. And the LORD had regard for Abel and his offering,

Noah
Genesis 8:20: Then Noah built an altar to the LORD and took some of every clean animal and some of every clean bird and offered burnt offerings on the altar.

Abraham
Genesis 22:13: And Abraham lifted up his eyes and looked, and behold, behind him was a ram, caught in a thicket by his horns. And Abraham went and took the ram and offered it up as a burnt offering instead of his son.

Israelites
Leviticus 1:3: If his offering is a burnt offering from the herd, he shall offer a male without blemish. He shall bring it to the entrance of the tent of meeting, that he may be accepted before the LORD.

The Law of Moses (i.e., Genesis–Deuteronomy) revealed sin as rebellion against God. The moral laws are summarized in the Ten Commandments (Exodus 20; Deuteronomy 5). Even with the Law, people continued rebelling and turning away from God (Romans 3:20). But God sent the ultimate and final sacrifice — far greater than any animal sacrifice — that would be sufficient to cover sin against a perfect God (Hebrews 10:1–14).

Jesus Christ, the Savior, Steps into History

John 3:16: For God so loved the world, that he gave his only Son, that whoever believes in him should not perish but have eternal life.

God sent His Son (i.e., the second person of the triune God[4]), Jesus, to humble Himself and enter into a sin-cursed world to live a servant's life on earth just like one of us (Philippians 2:8). He entered the world just as was prophesied — through the virgin Mary.

Jesus was without sin (1 John 3:5) and did everything perfectly according to the Law. Then, He would allow mankind to sacrifice Him on the Cross. Jesus would be the final sacrifice because He obeyed God completely and was without defect. Only He could satisfy the infinite punishment we deserve. His method of sacrifice (crucifixion) was even outlined many years before in Psalm 22. He was the perfect sacrifice (far exceeding the most perfect, unblemished animal) because He was the perfect man and also perfect God (Colossians 2:9).

Matthew 5:17: Do not think that I have come to abolish the Law or the Prophets; I have not come to abolish them but to fulfill them.

---

4. Mark Bird, "The Trinity," Answers in Genesis Website, July 30, 2008, online here: http://www.answersingenesis.org/articles/aid/v3/n1/the-trinity; Bodie Hodge, "God Is Triune," Answers in Genesis website, February 20, 2008, online here: http://www.answersingenesis.org/articles/2008/02/20/god-is-triune.

When God stepped into His creation, He offered what is called "grace." Grace, in essence, means that we were to be rightly punished for our wrongdoings, and then the One who sentenced us to that punishment took the punishment upon Himself because of love for us. We rightly deserved death by God's judgment, but God took that punishment upon Himself by dying in our place as Jesus Christ. He exercised that grace because of His love for us.

Jesus didn't come to the world to sentence it to death — the world was already condemned by sin. He came to save us from that sin. This indicates that God really is a God of love.

John 3:17–18: For God did not send his Son into the world to condemn the world, but in order that the world might be saved through him. Whoever believes in him is not condemned, but whoever does not believe is condemned already, because he has not believed in the name of the only Son of God.

Ephesians 2:1–7: And you were dead in the trespasses and sins in which you once walked, following the course of this world, following the prince of the power of the air, the spirit that is now at work in the sons of disobedience — among whom we all once lived in the passions of our flesh, carrying out the desires of the body and the mind, and were by nature children of wrath, like the rest of mankind. But God, being rich in mercy, because of the great love with which he loved us, even when we were dead in our trespasses, made us alive together with Christ — by grace you have been saved — and raised us up with him and seated us with him in the heavenly places in Christ Jesus, so that in the coming ages he might show the immeasurable riches of his grace in kindness toward us in Christ Jesus.

A second death is still the punishment that God will give to those who do not turn to Him. The second death is called hell and is separation from God — being completely separated from all that is good (Matthew 10:28, 23:33, 25:41–46). Even Satan himself has no power there. Jesus came to be the final sacrifice to allow us to be saved from this penalty due to sin against a holy God.

When Jesus rose and conquered death, people no longer needed to present an animal sacrifice to cover up their sins, for those who trust in Christ will receive the gift of the Holy Spirit. The Bible warns that the only unforgivable sin is blasphemy against the Holy Spirit. All other sins can be forgiven up to the moment of death.

> *Matthew 12:32:* And whoever speaks a word against the Son of Man will be forgiven, but whoever speaks against the Holy Spirit will not be forgiven, either in this age or in the age to come.

Blasphemy against the Holy Spirit is rejecting the Holy Spirit to the point of death.[5] The only way to reject the Holy Spirit is not receiving Jesus as your Savior during your lifetime. This corresponds to Jesus saying that He was the only way back to God the Father.

> *John 14:6:* Jesus said to him, "I am the way, and the truth, and the life. No one comes to the Father except through me.

The Free Gift of Salvation: Belief in Christ

Jesus, being the perfect sacrifice, offers the free gift of salvation. God loves you so much that He sacrificed His own unblemished Son to suffer the wrath against sin and die on the Cross. He commands

---

5　The greater context of Matthew 12:22–45 (also Mark 3:29 and Luke 12:10) (discussing spirit removal and their potential return) reveals that when Jesus cast out an evil spirit, the Pharisees accused Jesus of doing it by Beelzebub. They meant that it was "not by the Spirit of God." Take note that Jesus said this specific blasphemy would not be forgiven "in this age or the age to come" (vs. 32) but also later revealed they will "give an account on the day of judgment for their careless words" (vs. 36–37). On the flipside, Acts 13:39, Titus 2:14, 1 John 1:9, etc., reveal that believers are justified from "all things," from "every lawless deed," cleansed from "all unrighteousness," etc. Consider 1 John 1:7: "But if we walk in the light as he is in the light, we have fellowship with one another, and the blood of Jesus Christ His Son cleanses us from all sin." The only way both of these sets of Scriptures can be true is if people who utter such blasphemies (e.g., like the ones the Pharisees uttered) do not become believers.

you to repent (change your mind and turn from sinful ways) and trust in Him:

Ephesians 2:8–9: For by grace you have been saved through faith. And this is not your own doing; it is the gift of God, not a result of works, so that no one may boast.

2 Corinthians 7:10: For godly grief produces a repentance that leads to salvation without regret, whereas worldly grief produces death. (See also Mark 1:15; Luke 13:3–5; Acts 17:30.)

The Bible is clear in several passages how to receive salvation. It doesn't mean you are perfect after you are saved, but it does mean that you are perfectly forgiven and saved from the penalty of sin by God's grace.

John 3:16: For God so loved the world, that he gave his only Son, that whoever believes in him should not perish but have eternal life.

Acts 16:30–31: Then he brought them out and said, "Sirs, what must I do to be saved?" And they said, "Believe in the Lord Jesus, and you will be saved, you and your household."

Romans 10:9–10: . . . because, if you confess with your mouth that Jesus is Lord and believe in your heart that God raised him from the dead, you will be saved. For with the heart one believes and is justified, and with the mouth one confesses and is saved.

Mark 16:16: Whoever believes and is baptized will be saved, but whoever does not believe will be condemned.

These verses point out the importance of belief in Jesus Christ. It is a simple and free gift. It doesn't matter how many steps you've taken away from God; it is only one step back. If you are not a Christian, then consider more deeply the claims of Jesus, and please take a few minutes to pray to repent to God in the name of Jesus to forgive your sins and to receive Jesus Christ as the Lord of your life.

Encouragement

Our hope is that everyone who reads this will consider Jesus Christ as Lord and Savior. It is a powerful thing to be created by your Savior and yet saved by your Creator. A loving God created things perfectly and we, as fallen human beings, messed it up. And yet, He loved us so much that He stepped into history to save us by dying in our place

It would only be appropriate to love Him back. This is why Christians want to share this good news with others. Jesus said: *"If you love me, you will keep my commandments"* (John 14:15). Jesus said:

> *Matthew 28:18–20*: And Jesus came and said to them, "All authority in heaven and on earth has been given to me. Go therefore and make disciples of all nations, baptizing them in the name of the Father and of the Son and of the Holy Spirit, teaching them to observe all that I have commanded you. And behold, I am with you always, to the end of the age."

This is why Christians want to share the good news of salvation with others. We want them to come to know the love of God and get saved through Jesus Christ. And we want new Christians to continue learning about God by getting into God's Word, the Bible, and reading and learning what God has been so gracious to reveal to mankind.

If you prayed to receive Jesus Christ as your Lord and Savior, then please take some time to sit down with a Bible-believing pastor in a local church to help direct you as you begin your new life with Christ. Read your Bible every day and seek to understand and obey what you read. To God be the glory forever and ever.

Ten Basics to Boldly Proclaim a Biblical Worldview

Every Christian who stands unashamedly on the authority of God's Word should be ready to show how the Bible unlocks our understanding of the world. Yet certain questions seem to stump Christians more than other questions. Thankfully, when you accept the plain teaching of Scripture and build your thinking upon it, the basic answers are surprisingly simple. On the following pages are the nuts and bolts of the answers to ten of the most-asked questions that confuse Christians. More in-depth answers are readily available in resources written by creationist experts, but this is a great place to start. In this special series, highly qualified speakers and researchers with Answers in Genesis—USA have composed concise answers to each question, on a level anyone can understand.

Ten Basics Every Christian Must Know

1. Six literal days
2. Radiometric dating
3. Variety within created kinds
4. Uniqueness of man
5. Distant starlight
6. Global flood
7. Dinosaurs on the ark
8. One race
9. Suffering and death
10. The gospel

1. Six Literal Days

In the context, the word *day* in Genesis 1 refers to six 24-hour days. Every time it appears with "evening and morning" or with a number like "sixth day," it refers to a 24-hour day.

Did God create the whole universe, including the original plants, animals, and the first two people (Adam and Eve), in six literal 24-hour days? Or did creation take place over millions of years?

To answer that, we should remember that the original readers of Genesis were not scientists or Hebrew scholars. Rather, they were former slaves — mostly uneducated — on their way to the Promised Land. The fathers were commanded to teach their children (Deuteronomy 6:1–7), so the Hebrew language in Genesis 1 must have been very clear to the common people, even to children.

When we look carefully at Genesis 1, in Hebrew or even in English, it is clear that God created everything in six literal (24-hour) days. First, we are told that He created the earth in darkness and then created light. Then He called the light "day" and He called the darkness "night." And then He said (in the original Hebrew) "and [there] was evening and [there] was morning, one day." He repeated the same statement at the end of the second day through the sixth day.

And there was evening and there was morning, the sixth day (Genesis 1:31).

Everywhere else in the Old Testament, when the Hebrew word for "day" (*yom*) appears with "evening" or "morning" or is modified by a number (e.g., "sixth day" or "five days"), it always means a 24-hour day.

On day 4 God further showed that these were literal days by telling us the purpose for which He created the sun, moon, and stars — so we could tell time: literal years, literal seasons, and literal days.

Then in Exodus 20:8–11, God commanded the Israelites to work six literal "days" and rest on the seventh because He created in six "days" (using the same Hebrew word).

Furthermore, Jesus and the New Testament Apostles read Genesis 1–11 as straightforward historical narrative. There are additional good scholarly reasons for coming to that conclusion.

There is no biblical or scientific reason to be ashamed of believing in a recent six-day creation. God has spoken clearly and truthfully. Will you trust His Word over the arrogant claims of sinful men?

For Additional Information

+ Did Jesus Say He Created in Six Literal Days?[1]
+ Could God Really Have Created Everything in Six Days?[2]
+ Why Did God Take Six Days?[3]
+ Genesis Q & A[4]

Dr. Terry Mortenson is a well-known speaker, researcher, and writer for Answers in Genesis–USA. He earned his doctorate in history of geology from Coventry University in England, and he worked for Campus Crusade for Christ for 26 years. He also received his masters of divinity from Trinity Evangelical Divinity School in Chicago.

---

1. Ken Ham, editor, *The New Answers Book 1* (Green Forest, AR: Master Books, 2006), chapter 20.
2. Ibid., chapter 6.
3. http://www.answersingenesis.org/articles/2007/02/01/why-six-days.
4. http://www.answersingenesis.org/get-answers/topic/genesis.

2. Radiometric Dating

Does radiometric dating show that rocks are millions of years old? No! This dating method requires assumptions about the content of the original rocks and the decay rate in the past. Since the Bible is clear about the earth's age of thousands of years, the popular assumptions are wrong.

God's Word unmistakably teaches a young earth and universe ("the heavens"). God has ensured the accurate recording and preservation of His eyewitness account of the earth's history, which Jesus Christ endorsed repeatedly during His earthly ministry.

God took great care to include the necessary chronological details of the universe's creation in six literal days, as well as the unbroken genealogies of mankind from Adam to Jesus. So we have absolutely no doubt that the earth is only around six thousand years old.

Contrary to Scripture, many geologists claim that radiometric "clocks" show rocks to be millions of years old. However, to read any clock accurately we must know where the clock was set at the beginning. It's like making sure that an hourglass clock was set with all the sand in the top bowl at the beginning. However, no geologists were present when the earth and its many rock layers were formed, so they cannot know where the radiometric clocks were set at the beginning.

> Thus the heavens and the earth were finished, and all the host of them. And on the seventh day God finished His work (Genesis 2:1–2).

Also, we have to be sure that the clock has ticked at the same rate from the beginning until now. No geologists have been observing the radiometric clocks for millions of years to check that the rate of radioactive decay has always been the same as the rate today. To the contrary, we now have impeccable evidence that radioactive decay rates were greatly sped up at some point during the past, for example, during the global catastrophic Genesis Flood.

God is beyond time, which He created. He has told us when He created everything and thus how old the universe is. So we finite humans should fearlessly embrace His testimony of a young earth, recorded in His inerrant Word.

Wrong Assumptions, Wrong Dates

When scientists date rocks, they don't actually observe the atoms changing. They measure the products of the change, which they assume took place in the past. But what if they are wrong about their assumptions?

Assumption 1: The original number of unstable atoms in rocks isn't known. Scientists can measure only how many unstable and stable atoms remain in the rocks today.

Assumption 2: Scientists do not know how quickly unstable atoms decayed in the past. So they usually assume the atoms decayed as slowly as they do today.

For Additional Information

+ Radiometric Dating: Back to Basics[1]
+ Radiometric Dating: Problems with the Assumptions[2]
+ Does Radiometric Dating Prove the Earth Is Old?[3]
+ The Fallacies of Radioactive Dating of Rocks[4]
+ U-Th-Pb "Dating": An Example of False "Isochrons"[5]
+ Radiometric Dating Q & A[6]

1. http://www.answersingenesis.org/articles/am/v4/n3/radiometric-dating.
2. http://www.answersingenesis.org/articles/am/v4/n4/assumptions.
3. Ham, *The New Answers Book 1*, chapter 9.
4. http://www.answersingenesis.org/articles/am/v1/n1/radioactive-dating.
5. http://www.answersingenesis.org/articles/aid/v4/n1/false-isochrons.
6. http://www.answersingenesis.org/get-answers/topic/radiometric-dating.

Dr. Andrew Snelling holds a PhD in geology from the University of Sydney and has worked as a consultant research geologist to organizations in both Australia and America. He is the author of numerous scientific articles and is also director of research at Answers in Genesis—USA.

3. Variety within Created Kinds

Did all species evolve from one common ancestor? Genesis 1 repeats ten times that God created creatures separately according to various "kinds." Today's species show the potential variation that God designed within the original kinds, but this variety remains limited — cats are still cats, and dogs are dogs.

Our world is filled with a tremendous variety of life. And its origin is no mystery. The Bible says God created every kind of living thing on days 3, 5, and 6 of creation week. Ten times in Genesis 1 the phrase "according to its [or their] kind" is used in connection with different types of plants and animals. The word *kind* is used again in Genesis 6 when God instructed Noah to take two of every kind of land animal onto the ark; and in Genesis 8 God commanded these animals to reproduce after the Flood.

What does the word *kind* mean?

Since two of each *kind* of land animal (and seven of some) were brought aboard the ark for the purpose of preserving their offspring upon the earth (Genesis 7:3), it seems clear that a "kind" represents the basic reproductive boundary of an organism. That is, the offspring of an organism is always the same *kind* as its parents, even though it may display considerable variation.

Dogs, for example, exhibit tremendous variety. Yet diverse breeds of dogs can produce offspring with each other — indicating that all dogs are of the same *kind*. Dogs will not interbreed with cats, however, since they are a different kind. Modern breeding research therefore confirms the biblical concept of animal and plant kinds.

God made . . . everything . . . according to its kind (Genesis 1:25).

Creation researchers have found that "kind" is often at the level of "family" in our modern classification scheme. For example, zebras, horses, and donkeys all belong to the family Equidae and can mate with each other to form hybrid animals such as mules (from a horse and donkey) and zonkeys (from a zebra and donkey). However, there is no reason to assume a one-to-one correspondence between our manmade system and the biblical terminology. So "kind" may be at a higher taxonomic level in some cases, lower in others.

God placed the potential for tremendous variety within the original created kinds. This original variation, altered by genetic mutations and other mechanisms after the Fall (such as natural selection), led to the great diversity of living things we see today.

A modern field of study called baraminology (from the Hebrew words *bara*, meaning "created," and *min*, meaning "kind") attempts to classify fossil and living organisms into their original created kinds (or baramins). This is an active area of creation research. As creation scientists, we are not ashamed to stand on the foundation of God's Word for our research and understanding of living things.

For Additional Information

+ Rapid Speciation (Video)[1]
+ Zonkeys, Ligers, and Wolphins, Oh My![2]
+ Bara-What?[3]
+ Creation's Hidden Potential[4]
+ Created Kinds (Baraminology) Q & A[5]

Dr. Georgia Purdom earned her doctorate from Ohio State University in molecular genetics and spent six years as a professor of biology at Mt. Vernon Nazarene University. Dr. Purdom is also a member of the American Society for Microbiology and American Society for Cell Biology.

1. http://www.answersingenesis.org/articles/am/v3/n4/rapid-speciation.
2. http://www.answersingenesis.org/articles/aid/v3/n1/zonkeys-ligers-wholphins.
3. http://www.answersingenesis.org/articles/am/v3/n4/bara-what.
4. http://www.answersingenesis.org/articles/am/v4/n1/hidden-potential.
5. http://www.answersingenesis.org/get-answers/topic/created-kinds.

4. Uniqueness of Man

Genesis 1 states that God specially created the first male and female in His own image. Jesus Christ restated that the first couple were created "at the beginning," not from apes. Despite some anatomical similarities among all mammals, it is easy to distinguish humans.

Perhaps the most offensive feature of evolutionism to Bible-believing Christians is the belief that humans have evolved by natural processes from apes. In the evolutionary view, moreover, man was not the goal of evolution but a mere happenstance. This stands in startling contrast to the biblical declaration that humans were specially created in the image of God.

God created man in His own image (Genesis 1:27).

In the first chapter of Genesis, the triune God declared, " 'Let us make man in our image, after our likeness. And let them have dominion over the fish of the sea and over the birds of the heavens and over the lievestock and over all the earth and over every creeping thing that creeps on the earth.' So God created man in his own image, in the image of God he created him; male and female he created them" (Genesis 1:26–27). Far from being an evolutionary descendant of the beasts, man has been given dominion over them.

Jesus directed our attention to the second chapter of Genesis when He said, "Have you not read that he who created them from the beginning made them male and female, and said, 'Therefore a man shall leave his father and his mother and hold fast to his wife, and the two shall become one flesh'?" (Matthew 19:4–5).

Since God did not create any "ape men," it should come as no surprise that it is quite easy to distinguish humans from apes, whether as fossils or living. While there is an underlying anatomical similarity among all mammals, a child can be taught to recognize the difference between an ape skull and that of a human.

But it is not the biological differences (anatomical or physiological) that definitively set man apart from the beasts. Rather, the mind and soul of man and his God-given ability to communicate with our Creator distance him from the beasts. Thus, it is only mankind that is invited to join the Apostle Paul in declaring, "For I am not ashamed of the gospel, for it is the power of God for salvation to everyone who believes" (Romans 1:16).

For Additional Information

+ Did Humans Really Evolve from Apelike Creatures?[6]
+ The Human Kind[7]
+ Apemen & Missing Links Q & A[8]

Dr. David Menton holds his PhD in cell biology from Brown University and is a well-respected author and teacher. He is Professor Emeritus at the Washington University School of Medicine in St. Louis. Dr. Menton has many published works and is one of the most popular speakers for Answers in Genesis–USA.

6. Ken Ham, editor, *The New Answers Book 2* (Green Forest, AR: Master Books, 2008), chapter 8; also http://www.answersingenesis.org/articles/nab2/humans-evolve-apelike-creatures.

7. Ken Ham and A. Charles Ware, *One Race, One Blood* (Green Forest, AR: Master Books, 2010), chapter 4; also http://www.answersingenesis.org/PublicStore/product/One-Race-One-Blood,6724,224.aspx.

8. http://www.answersingenesis.org/get-answers#/topic/apemen-missing-links.

5. Distant Starlight

Can stars be millions of light years away if God created them only 6,000 years ago? We have much to learn, but several astrophysical models can account for this. Interestingly, the big bang has a major light-travel problem of its own.

Sometimes Christians are reluctant to discuss the age of the universe. The Bible states that God created in six days, and its genealogies clearly indicate that this took place only a few thousand years ago. But some people reason, "Hasn't science demonstrated that it would take billions of years for the light from the farthest galaxies to reach the earth? Doesn't this disprove the Genesis account or force us to interpret the words differently?"

Not at all.

There are several known ways that light can travel vast distances in a relatively short period of time. In fact, Einstein tells us that if a person could travel at the speed of light, then the trip would be completely instantaneous (from his or her point of view). It takes literally no time at all to travel from a distant galaxy to the earth as far as the light is concerned.

There are several ways to accomplish this instant trip from the earth's point of view as well. Time-dilation models, for example, use Einstein's physics to get light here in a short period of time, at least from the earth's perspective.

God made . . . the stars . . . [on] the fourth day (Genesis 1:16–19).

Perhaps most promising is a newer model that uses an alternative way to synchronize two clocks that are far apart. Much like a plane can leave Kentucky at 4:00 and arrive in Colorado at 4:00 because of different time zones, so starlight could arrive on earth on day 4, regardless of how far away the star is.

We should also remember that God is not limited to natural methods as we are.

Ironically, the leading secular alternative to the Bible (the big bang) has a light-travel time problem of its own. Known as the "horizon problem," the big bang is unable to get light from one side of the universe to the other within its own billions-of-years time frame.[2] To alleviate this problem, big-bang supporters must arbitrarily add another hypothesis like "inflation" (which has problems of its own).

Even if our current creation models turn out to be wrong, there is no need to be embarrassed by distant starlight, for we rely upon the revealed Word of God as our starting point. Unlike the shifting opinions of men, such a foundation cannot fail. It boldly declares that on day 4 "God made . . . the stars" (Genesis 1:16).

For Additional Information

+ Deflating Billions of Years[1]
+ Straight Answers to Common Questions[2]
+ Does Distant Starlight Prove the Universe Is Old?[3]
+ The Age of the Universe, Part 1[4]

> Dr. Jason Lisle holds a PhD in astrophysics from University of Colorado at Boulder and is a popular speaker for Answers in Genesis–USA. Dr. Lisle uses his knowledge of the heavens and his biblical perspective to proclaim the handiwork of God in lectures, including Distant Starlight and Creation Astronomy.

---

1. http://www.answersingenesis.org/get-answers/features/billions-of-years.

2. http://www.answersingenesis.org/articles/am/v3/n1/straight-answers-common-questions.

3. Ham, *The New Answers Book 1*, chapter 19; also http://www.answersingenesis.org/articles/nab/does-starlight-prove.

4. Jason Lisle, *Taking Back Astronomy* (Green Forest, AR: Master Books, 2009), chapter 3; also http://www.answersingenesis.org/articles/tba/age-of-the-universe-1.

6. Global Flood

Did Noah experience a local flood that left only a few sediment layers, as floods do today? God's record is clear: the water covered the entire globe and killed all the land-dwelling, air-breathing animals on earth, as well as many other marine animals. Such unique conditions are the best way to explain worldwide fossil-bearing layers thousands of feet deep.

Scripture is clear about the historic reality of a global Flood in Noah's day. Genesis 7:19–22 specifically says that water covered all the high hills by 26 feet (15 cubits or 8 m), and all air-breathing land animals and people that were outside the ark died.

Today, many people unfortunately do not accept the biblical account of a worldwide Flood because they have been taught that most rocks and fossils were deposited over millions of years (and therefore not by a global Flood). Until the 1800s, most Westerners believed what the Bible records about the earth's recent creation and the global Flood. The secular idea of millions of years did not catch fire until the 1830s, under the influence of a man named Charles Lyell.

The waters prevailed so mightily on the earth that all the high mountains under the whole heaven were covered (Genesis 7:19).

Based on how slowly rock layers usually form today, Lyell rejected the Bible's claims and declared that the earth's many rock layers must have been laid down slowly over millions of years. But he never witnessed the actual formation of the earlier rocks to see whether they could be laid by a unique, one-time global Flood unlike anything we observe today. Lyell's claim was based on his own preconceptions, not his observations.

Yet his idea took hold in Western universities and spread throughout the Western world. Sadly, many Christians simply tried to add this idea to the Bible. What these Christians should have done was stand on the authority of the Bible and defend the global Flood, which can easily account for the bulk of fossil-bearing rock layers we find all over the world.

Although there is tremendous physical evidence of a global Flood, ultimately, it is a matter of trust in a perfect God who created everything (Genesis 1:1), knows everything (Colossians 2:3), has always been there (Revelation 22:13), and cannot lie (Titus 1:2). The only alternative is to trust imperfect, fallible human beings who can only speculate on the past (see Romans 3:4).

Some Christians have tried to put millions of years of rock formation before the global Flood to explain the bulk of the rock layers that contain fossils. But the problem is that the Flood waters could rip up many of the previous rock layers and redeposit them elsewhere! So this compromise not only fails to explain the rock layers but also dishonors the clear claims of Scripture.

A global Flood makes perfect sense, and it is wrong and foolish to stray from God's Word just because some men disagree.

For Additional Information

+ Flood Legends[1]
+ Universality of the Genesis Flood[2]
+ Geologic Evidences for the Genesis Flood[3]
+ Was There Really a Noah's Ark & Flood?[4]
+ Flood Q & A[5]

Bodie Hodge earned both his undergraduate and master's degrees from Southern Illinois at Carbondale in mechanical engineering. Bodie is now a speaker and writer at Answers in Genesis–USA.

1. http://www.answersingenesis.org/articles/am/v2/n2/flood-legends.
2. http://www.answersingenesis.org/articles/am/v2/n2/universality-of-flood.
3. http://www.answersingenesis.org/articles/am/v2/n4/geologic-evidences-part-one.
4. Ham, *The New Answers Book 1*, chapter 10; also http://www.answersingenesis.org/articles/nab/really-a-flood-and-ark.
5. http://www.answersingenesis.org/get-answers#/topic/flood.

7. Dinosaurs on the Ark

Did dinosaurs really live at the same time as humans? Genesis 1 claims that God created every "kind" of land animal on the same day as Adam. Later Noah took representatives of every kind on the ark. That required only about 50 dinosaur kinds on board. (Dinosaurs are divided into only about 50 families.)

Dinosaurs are used more than any other animal to persuade people to believe in millions of years and evolution. Yet God clearly claims that He created the land animals on day 6 along with man. In light of who God is and His eyewitness testimony, we should not be ashamed to build our understanding of dinosaurs upon His Word, even if some people disagree. Dinosaurs make perfect sense in light of the biblical history of creation and the Flood.

There are thousands of dinosaur names, so some skeptics ask, "How could two of every kind of dinosaur fit on the ark?" The key to unlocking the answer is found in Genesis 7:14–15.

The Bible states that two of every kind of land animal and seven of some went onto the ark. It doesn't say two of every species went onto the ark, but "kinds." There are thousands of species of dinosaurs, but there are only about 50 families of dinosaurs. And since the biblical kind is thought to correspond to the family level in most cases, there would have been only about 100 dinosaurs on the ark — not thousands.

> Every beast according to its kind . . . went into the ark with Noah, two by two (Genesis 7:14–15).

For instance, the long-neck sauropods include many different species, such as *Brachiosaurus*, *Camarasaurus*, *Saltasaurus*, and *Diplodocus*, but only two of this kind needed to go onto the ark. This fact dramatically reduces the estimated number of dinosaurs on the ark. Also, even though some dinosaurs grew to be large creatures, the average size was only about the size of a large sheep or bison. Even the largest dinosaurs were quite small when hatched. The Lord may have selected younger (and therefore smaller) representatives of some of the larger kinds, so there was plenty of room for all of the dinosaur kinds aboard the ark.

If dinosaurs sailed on the ark, where are they today? Different animal species become extinct every day for various reasons. After the Flood, the environment and habitat were drastically changed. Many dinosaurs may not have been as suited to the post-Flood world because of these changes. Interestingly, it appears that some of the dinosaur kinds that did survive a long time after the Flood became known as dragons. Dragon legends abound all over the world.

We can confidently build our understanding of dinosaurs — like everything else in life — on the truth of God's Word.

For Additional Information

+ What Really Happened to the Dinosaurs?[1]
+ Dinosaur Killer[2]
+ Why Don't We Find Human & Dinosaur Fossils Together?[3]
+ Were Dinosaurs on Noah's Ark?[4]
+ Dinosaurs Q & A[5]

> *Buddy Davis is one of children's favorite Answers in Genesis–USA speakers. He travels extensively conducting workshops for kids, teaching them how to defend their faith. He is not only a renowned musician and "paleo-artist," but he is also an adventurer, joining expeditions to places like Alaska and Turkey searching for dinosaur fossils and Noah's ark.*

1. Ham, *The New Answers Book 1*, chapter 12; also http://www.answersingenesis.org/articles/nab/what-happened-to-the-dinosaurs.
2. http://www.answersingenesis.org/articles/am/v3/n1/dinosaur-killer.
3. Ham, *The New Answers Book 1*, chapter 13; http://www.answersingenesis.org/articles/nab/human-and-dino-fossils-together.
4. http://www.answersingenesis.org/articles/2000/04/03/dinosaurs-on-noahs-ark.
5. http://www.answersingenesis.org/get-answers#/topic/dinosaurs.

8. One Race

Over the last several decades, many examples of fraternal twins, where one is very dark (called "black") and one very light (called "white"), have been documented. Documented examples of fraternal twins being "black" and "white" include:

1. The Hodgson-Horder twin girls (born April 2005 in England)
2. The Biggs twin girls (born July 2006 in Australia)
3. The Richardson twin boys (born July 2006 in England)
4. The Grant twin girls (born 1983 in England)
5. The Singerl twin girls (born May 2006 in Australia)

Some of the parents of these sets of twins have shared that people stopped and stared when they saw the "black" and "white" children. But in reality, such sets of twins are quite easy to explain and should not invoke such responses. So how can such "black" and "white" twins — though quite rare — be explained?

According to the Bible's history, all humans are descendants of Adam and Eve — thus only one biological race exists. All humans in the world today are classified as *Homo sapiens sapiens* (same genus, species, and subspecies). When the Human Genome Project published a draft of their findings in 2000, the *New York Times* reported that "the researchers had unanimously declared there is only one race — the human race."[1]

To form different people groups with distinguishing characteristics, one would need to split up the human population and isolate groups from each other. The Tower of Babel, as recorded in Genesis 11, provides the historical basis for the formation of such people groups. There is so much information in the human genome that zillions of combinations are possible.

---

1. Natalie Angier, "Do Races Differ? Not Really, Genes Show," *New York Times*, August 22, 2000.

Yet all humans basically have the same skin color — a brown pigment called *melanin*. Although there are a couple of forms of melanin and other pigments and factors playing minor roles in skin color, every human basically has a brown color.

Lots of brown is called *black*, and a little brown color is called *white*. In actuality, no human really is "black" and no human is "white." There are not different colors but different shades of one basic color, brown.

While many factors are involved in determining skin color and the steps are very technical, basic genetics can help us understand the most important principles.

Assume dominant genes result in lots of melanin and recessive genes result in little melanin. Adam and Eve were most likely a middle brown color with both dominant and recessive genes for the pigment melanin in the skin. Children who received all the dominant genes would end up with a lot of the color and be very dark. Children who received all the recessive genes would end up with only a little color and be very light. Children with a mixture of the genes (both dominant and recessive) would be middle brown.

So it's not just "black" and "white." The bottom line is, a person's skin shade (what is on the outside) should in no way invoke any sort of prejudice or racist comments. What a difference we would see in our world if people reacted in accord with biblical principles, understanding all humans are equal before God, and all are sinners in need of salvation. All of us need to build our thinking on the absolute authority of the Word of God, judging all beliefs and attitudes against the clear teaching of what our Creator God teaches us.

God reminded Samuel of this when He said, "For the LORD sees not as man sees: man looks on the outward appearance, but the LORD looks on the heart" (1 Samuel 16:7).

For Additional Information

+ Are There Really Different Races?[1]
+ One Race, One Blood[2]
+ Darwin and Lincoln[3]
+ Darwin's Sacred Cause?[4]
+ Racism Q & A[5]

Ken Ham is the president/CEO and founder of Answer in Genesis-U.S. and the highly acclaimed Creation Museum. He is also one of the most in-demand Christian speakers in North America. Ham, a native Australian, now resides near Cincinnati, Ohio, and is the author of numerous best-selling books. Ken hosts the daily radio program, "Answers . . . with Ken Ham," heard on more than 800 stations in America (and dozens more overseas) and is one of the editors and contributing authors for AiG's Answers *magazine (a biblical worldview publication with over 70,000 worldwide subscribers).*

1. Ham, *The New Answers Book 1*, chapter 17; also http://www.answersingenesis.org/articles/nab/are-there-different-races.
2. Ham and Ware, *One Race, One Blood*; also http://www.answersingenesis.org/PublicStore/product/One-Race-One-Blood,6724,224.aspx.
3. http://www.answersingenesis.org/articles/2009/02/12/darwin-and-lincoln.
4. http://www.answersingenesis.org/articles/2009/04/07/darwins-sacred-cause.
5. http://www.answersingenesis.org/get-answers/topic/racism.

9. Suffering and Death

If God is so good, why is this world filled with suffering and death? The answer is plainly described in Genesis 1–3. God created a "very good" world, but Adam's rebellion brought a curse and death. The disease and death in the fossil record reflect this curse.

Why do people suffer? Why do people die? Isn't this a horrible world we live i n?

These questions vex not only the unbeliever but the believer as well. Yet as is true in every other question, we should not be ashamed to stand on the authority of God's Word to understand death and suffering.

This question is not as difficult as it might seem. A person only needs to open the Bible and read Genesis chapters 1–3 to find the answer. Here we are told of the beginning of things — God created everything in six ordinary days. We read of a perfect creation in which there was no death. God looked at His creation and called it "very good" (Genesis 1:31).

So where did death come from?

Death came as a direct result of Adam's disobedience. Genesis 2:17 tells us, "But of the tree of the knowledge of good and evil you shall not eat, for in the day that you eat of it you shall surely die." So Adam knew there was a consequence to his actions. When he took of the fruit and ate, death entered God's perfect creation. "For since by man came death, by Man also came the resurrection of the dead" (1 Corinthians 15:21).

Because you . . . have eaten of the tree . . . cursed is the ground . . . and to dust you shall return (Genesis 3:17–19).

Our world is broken, marred by death and suffering. We must understand that our sin is what broke God's perfect creation. The suffering in this world is the first Adam's fault, the consequence of his disobedience to a holy God. We are all sinners because we are descended from sinners and we, too, rebel against God's command (Romans 5:12). Not one is innocent. As a result of sin, "The whole creation has been groaning together in the pains of childbirth until now" (Romans 8:22).

The good news is that the Last Adam, Jesus Christ, came to earth to bear the penalty of our sins and be nailed to the Cross. He defeated death by His Resurrection. By His atoning blood sacrifice for us, He has made a way for us to spend eternity with Him in heaven. Further, He promised to those who place their faith in Him that in the future there will be no more death, tears, or suffering.

The perfect world will then be restored.

For More Information

+ Why Does God's Creation Include Death & Suffering?[6]
+ Evil at God's Hand[7]
+ Why Do God's Children Suffer?[8]
+ How Could a Loving God?[9]
+ Death and Suffering Q & A[10]

> *Dr. Tommy Mitchell, a Fellow of the American College of Physicians, earned his MD from Vanderbilt University School of Medicine and practiced medicine for over 20 years. He is now a researcher and speaker at Answers in Genesis–USA.*

6. Ham, *The New Answers Book 1*, chapter 26; also http://www.answersingenesis.org/articles/nab/why-does-creation-include-suffering.

7. http://www.answersingenesis.org/articles/am/v4/n3/evil.

8. http://www.answersingenesis.org/articles/am/v4/n3/children-suffer.

9. Ken Ham, *How Could a Loving God. . . ?* (Green Forest, AR: Master Books, 2007); also http://www.answersingenesis.org/articles/hcalg

10. http://www.answersingenesis.org/get-answers/topic/death-suffering.

10. The Gospel

Christians who stand confidently on the Bible's historical record have the answer to life's troubles. The Creator of our once-perfect world promised to become our Savior. Born in the line of Abram, Jesus Christ suffered death so He could offer life to all who trust Him.

A turning point in history occurred when God said to Abram, "And in you all the families of the earth shall be blessed" (Genesis 12:3). God promised Abram (soon to be renamed "Abraham") that in his seed all the nations of the earth would be blessed.

The bottom line of this reference is the work of the Messiah (Jesus Christ), the promised descendant of Abraham. He lived a perfect life, died on a Cross for our sins, and rose again, offering life to all who believe in Him (1 Corinthians 15:1–4).

This gospel must be the focus of any Christian's ministry. The ultimate goal of ministry is not simply winning debates but proclaiming the gospel.

As stated in Answers in Genesis's statement of faith, "The scientific aspects of creation are important but are secondary in importance to the proclamation of the gospel of Jesus Christ as Sovereign, Creator, Redeemer, and Judge."

In you [Abram] all the families of the earth shall be blessed (Genesis 12:3).

Christians can use arguments to help break down "strongholds" (2 Corinthians 10:4), but the end result must be to fill the void with the truth that leads to salvation. Just knowledge of facts will not save anyone. The power is not in any human reasoning but in God's Word and Christ's work. Jesus is the way, the truth, and the life (John 14:6). No other name, no amount of persuasiveness, and no eloquence can save anyone.

All the treasures of wisdom and knowledge are found in Christ (Colossians 2:3).

Christians are told to be ready always to give an answer (1 Peter 3:15). Answers to technical questions can show how the Bible is relevant, encourage confidence in God's Word, and strengthen believers, but these answers are only a step in evangelizing the lost.

Christians must study to show themselves approved, rightly handling the Word of God (2 Timothy 2:15). We should not be ashamed to give the message of the gospel to anyone, no matter how intellectual or anti-Bible they may seem.

And never forget, the gospel begins in Genesis!

For Additional Information

+ The Gospel of Jesus Christ[1]
+ What *is* the Gospel?[2]
+ How Can I Use This Information to Witness?[3]
+ Declaring God's Glory Among the Nations[4]
+ Does Church Need Change?[5]

Mike Riddle, a former captain in the U.S. Marine Corps, is a well-known creation speaker for Answers in Genesis–USA. He holds a BS in mathematics and an MS in education. Mike was also a world-class decathlon athlete and a US national track-and-field pentathlon champion.

1. http://www.answersingenesis.org/about/good-news.
2. Ken Ham, *Why Won't They Listen?* (Green Forest, AR: Master Books, 2002), chapter 2; also http://www.answersingenesis.org/home/Area/WWTL/chapter2.asp.
3. Ham *The New Answer Book 1*, chapter 27; also http://www.answersingenesis.org/articles/nab/how-use-information-to-witness.
4. http://www.answersingenesis.org/articles/am/v2/n4/declaring-gods-glory.
5. http://www.answersingenesis.org/articles/am/v4/n4/church-change.

A Final Note of Truth: Wasn't the Bible Written by Mere Men?

All Scripture is breathed out by God and profitable for teaching, for reproof, for correction, and for training in righteousness, that the man of God may be competent, equipped for every good work (2 Timothy 3:16–17).

I didn't realize how important this question was until I saw a statistic of young people who had walked away from the church. Out of 1,000 young adults surveyed who have left church, 44 percent of them said that they did not believe the accounts in the Bible were true and accurate. When asked what made them answer this way, the most common response (24 percent) was that the Bible was written by men. Some of the results from that 44 percent are listed below.[1]

- 24 percent — it was written by men
- 18 percent — it was not translated correctly
- 15 percent — the Bible contradicts itself
- 11 percent — the Bible has errors

Even though 24 percent directly claimed this, take note that there are related answers such as 11 percent believing the Bible to have errors, which means God could not have been involved since God does not make errors (Psalm 12:6; Deuteronomy 32:4). Also, claiming that the Bible contradicts itself would imply that God was not involved since God cannot deny Himself (2 Timothy 2:13), and thus contradict Himself. So at least 50 percent would, in one way or another, dispute that a perfect God was responsible for the Bible!

1. Ken Ham and Britt Beemer, *Already Gone* (Green Forest, AR: Master Books, 2009), p. 107.

So What Is the Answer?

When it comes to the authorship of the Bible, of course men were involved — Christians would be the first to point this out. Paul wrote letters to early churches and these became Scripture. David wrote many of the Psalms, Moses wrote the Pentateuch (the first five books of the Bible), and so on. In fact, it is estimated that over 40 different human authors were involved.[2] So this is not the real issue.

The real issue is whether God had any involvement in the authorship of the Bible. Let's think about this for a moment. When someone claims that the Bible was written by men *and not God*, this is an absolute statement that reveals something extraordinary. It reveals that the person saying this is claiming to be transcendent! For a person to validate the claim that God did not inspire the human authors of the Bible means he must be omniscient, omnipresent, and omnipotent!

So the person making the claim that the Bible was merely written by men is claiming to be God, since these three attributes belong to God alone. This is ultimately a religious issue of humanism versus Christianity. People who make such claims (perhaps unwittingly) are claiming that *they* are the ultimate authority over God and are trying to convince others that God is *subservient* to them.

What Is a Good Response?

I like to respond to this claim with a question that reveals this real issue — and there are several ways to do this. Ask them a question like "How do you know that God was not involved?" But then you will have to listen carefully to the response to know how to respond after that.

Another response would be to point out that any type of reasoning apart from the Bible is merely arbitrary. So the person trying to make a logical argument against the claims of the Bible (i.e., that God inspired the authors) is doing so only because he or she is assuming

2. Josh McDowell, *A Ready Defense* (Nashville, TN: Thomas Nelson Publishers, 1993), p. 27.

(though unintentionally) the Bible is true and that logic and truth exist! It is good to point out these types of presuppositions and inconsistencies.[3]

Conclusion

Sadly, in today's society, people, whether churched or not, are being heavily exposed to the religion of humanism. This religion reigns in state schools and is creeping into the Church. So it is logical that people are thinking in terms of humanism and applying that to their view of the Bible.

You shall have no other gods before me (Exodus 20:3).

If one can understand, expose, and respond to the false religion of humanism, then unbelievers may be more open to realizing that they are being deceived, and Christians will have a stronger understanding of God's Word.

Bodie Hodge is on the staff of Answers in Genesis, and is a speaker, writer, and researcher on a host of topics, including Genesis, scriptural authority, the fall of Satan, and related events.

3. Jason Lisle, "Feedback: Put the Bible Down," Answers in Genesis, www.answersingenesis.org/articles/2008/12/05/feedback-put-the-bible-down.

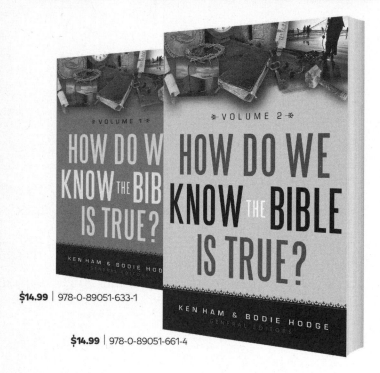

Connect with Master Books®

Ken Ham

📶 nlpgblogs.com

f facebook.com/masterbooks

t @masterbooks4u

You Tube youtube.com/nlpgvideo

Connect with Ken Ham

📶 blogs.answersingenesis.org

f facebook.com/aigkenham

t @aigkenham

Bodie Hodge

Connect with Creation Museum

creationmuseum.org

f facebook.com/creationmuseum

t @creationmuseum

Connect with Answers in Genesis

answersingenesis.org

f facebook.com/answersingenesis

t @aig